TRANSFORMATIVE LEISURE

Annette M. Holba

TRANSFORMATIVE LEISURE

A PHILOSOPHY OF COMMUNICATION

MARQUETTE
UNIVERSITY
PRESS

MARQUETTE STUDIES IN PHILOSOPHY
NO. 82
ANDREW TALLON, SERIES EDITOR

© 2013 Marquette University Press
Milwaukee, Wisconsin 53201-3141
All rights reserved.
www.marquette.edu/mupress/

LIBRARY OF CONGRESS CATALOGING-IN-PUBLICATION DATA

Holba, Annette, 1960-
Transformative leisure : a philosophy of communication / Annette M. Holba. — first [edition].
    pages cm. — (Marquette studies in philosophy ; No. 82)
Includes bibliographical references and index.
ISBN 978-0-87462-717-6 (pbk. : alk. paper) — ISBN 0-87462-717-6 (pbk. : alk. paper)
1. Leisure—Philosophy. I. Title.
GV14.H643 2013
790.01—dc23

2013015060

Cover Design by Coco Connolly cocoxoxo.com

♾ The paper used in this publication meets the minimum requirements of the American National Standard for Information Sciences—Permanence of Paper for Printed Library Materials, ANSI Z39.48-1992.

Association of American University Presses

MARQUETTE UNIVERSITY PRESS
MILWAUKEE

The Association of Jesuit University Presses

To

Francois Marie Pupunat
Lausanne, Switzerland (1858)

Je vous remercie de me donner de loisirs

CONTENTS

ACKNOWLEDGEMENTS

LOOKING BACK—LOOKING AHEAD—
LOOKING BEYOND

I t was in my first year of doctoral studies at Duquesne University that I discovered a small book with a title that caught my attention, *Leisure: The Basis of Culture*, written by Josef Pieper in 1948 and reprinted in 1998. My discovery occurred after a particular conversation I had with my professor and mentor, Ronald C. Arnett. After my first semester of course work I had serious doubts about whether or not I could successfully complete the program. While I have since completed the program, that little book changed my approach to daily living in that it opened up to me a world that I intuitively knew even though I had not yet developed the vocabulary to talk about it. I read the book over the semester break and at the end of the spring semester of my first year of doctoral studies I presented a paper in a colloquia series which would later become the topic of my dissertation, numerous paper presentations at academic conventions, several journal articles, and two books (this being the second book). What I had discovered through my readings and my mentoring was that the human community was missing something that would have devastating consequences if left unattended. I decided to pursue the question of transformative leisure, the lack of transformative leisure in our lives, and search for reasons why human beings might resist the idea of transformative leisure in popular culture.

In short, and I hope that after reading the following chapters, the significance of transformative leisure in our lives will be unraveled in such a way that your perception of leisure and your experience with leisure will be altered. Since transformative leisure cultivates the ground upon which one engages others in communicative action, interaction, and transaction, it is important that we hear this call and situate the formal study of transformative leisure as a priority.

WORDS OF GRATITUDE

Acknowledgments are sometimes difficult to formalize. There have been so many people, perhaps too numerous to count, who have had some kind of impact on my thinking about transformative leisure over the years. So, while this could never be an exhaustive list, these people and particular circumstances have had significant influence in my thinking and in my writing. First, I begin with Ramsey Eric Ramsey who has encouraged me to find my own voice when it comes to thinking, writing, and speaking/presenting my ideas about transformative leisure. In particular, I refer to an invitation that came from Ramsey Eric Ramsey, Associate Dean for Arizona State University, The Barrett Honors College. In February 2011 I traveled to Barrett Honors College in Phoenix, AZ after accepting an invitation to speak about transformative leisure and food to both undergraduate and graduate students. During my visit I had multiple opportunities to chat with Ramsey Eric, his colleagues, and ASU Barrett students and I learned that there are multiple ways of articulating philosophical positions but that each position should be crafted in an individual scholarly voice that tends to concepts, terms, and possibilities beyond assumptions of what has already been said. Through numerous fortuitous conversations, Ramsey Eric encouraged me to find my own voice that transcends beyond the voice of what already is. It is from these kinds of experiences that initially appear uncertain and unknown, we can make remarkable choices and movement toward the not-yet—I have truly learned a great deal from our discussions.

I also want to thank Ronald C. Arnett for his continued support and encouragement of my scholarly interests—I've learned most about otherness, beyond my expectations, through our scholarly and professional collaborations. I also want to thank Pat Arneson who has supported me professionally and personally. Janie Harden Fritz, as well, has been incredibly supportive and a good friend. Michael J. Hyde's friendship, work, and genuine humanness have touched me in ways that continue to validate my existence and presence in the academy. Finally, writing about leisure philosophically began with my first book on leisure that was published by Marquette University Press in 2007, *Philosophical leisure: Recuperative Praxis for Human Communication*. The series editor, Andrew Tallon, has taught me about grace, voice, and commitment in academia through that first publication experience—he gave me the opportunity of a lifetime to use my naïve voice in a way that was worthy of contributing to an ongoing conversation about leisure, philosophy, and our human condition. His professional nudges have been instructive, insightful, and have remained with me in my other publishing experiences. You are all such good friends, colleagues, and mentors—I am honored to know each of you.

I'd also like to thank Julie Bernier, Provost and Vice President of Academic Affairs at Plymouth State University and Sara Jayne Steen, President of Plymouth State University, for giving me great support in my personal and professional experience here at Plymouth State University. I'd like to thank Lisbeth Lipari who, through a response to a panel discussion at NCA in 2009, made a statement that included the phrase, hermeneutic humility, which ultimately helped to shift the focus of this project early on. As incredible as it seems, that panel response has played a profoundly significant role in my development of transformative leisure. I also attended several conferences and conventions where I was able to test and cultivate my ideas, which include the National Communication Association Annual Convention (2009); the Eastern Communication Association Annual Convention (2010 and 2011); and the National Communication Ethics Summer Conference at Duquesne University (2010). I'd like to especially thank Cem Zeytinoglu for helping me work through some ideas pertaining to the philosophy of Karl Marx, I genuinely enjoyed our convention discussions and I hope they continue throughout the years.

In order to write a book while one is teaching a full course load, it becomes important to thank my family. First, to my husband, Dan, you are a gift, thank you for doing everything so that I could write this book, our time is coming. To our sixteen year old dog, Emily, thank you for your patience when you really had to go outside but you let me finish a sentence (or two...or three) before I'd take you out. Thank you dad, it was good to watch you carve your ducks, birds, dolphins, and Woody Woodpeckers while I sat at my computer typing my book. Thank you Sandra Anderson Decarie, my friend, who had the arduous task of reading the first manuscript draft while playing with Ian on your farm. Your comments were very helpful. Finally, thank you to our five children and four grandchildren who sometimes get caught up in the everyday nitty gritty and we (Dan and me), as parents and grandparents, can ask them to sit back and recapture transformative leisure in their lives—they owe it to the other.

INTRODUCTION

. . . cultivated leisure . . .and not labour, is the aim of man

—Oscar Wilde

For all of his arch wit, Oscar Wilde is also quite serious—our aim ought to be leisure. This must strike the contemporary ear with a harshness. Wilde gives us a recipe for a good life and in doing so anticipates Josef Piepers' invitation to regain leisure in our lives. Wilde points us in the direction of what he understands is a normative condition for living life that aims us toward possibilities inherent to what it means to be human. In all of our seeking outside of ourselves to find meaning in our existence with others, Wilde's insight takes us back home in some kind of urgency. The way home comes through leisure as it points us to an ethical understanding of ourselves.

Wilde's passage, in it fullness, "Humanity will be amusing itself, or enjoying cultivated leisure, which—and not labour, is the aim of man—or making beautiful things, reading beautiful things, or simply contemplating the world with admiration and delight" points us home, away from a massification of industry so that we can return to live better in the world of things.[1] The idea of cultivation implies attending to something with our minds and our hands, perhaps in the philosophical spirit of *poiesis*. For Wilde, leisure appears oppositional to labour, though labour can be a complex concept. If we consider labour in the sense that Arendt considered labour, we understand that labour is life-giving and life-sustaining. Wilde conflates Arendt's notion of labour and work; labour as life-giving and sustaining and work as a work-a-day toil for one's living that sustains one materialistically but not spiritually. The aim then, as Wilde so aptly puts it, is to attend to the world in a way that is driven by admiration and delight in a

---

1   Oscar Wilde, *The Soul of Man under Socialism and Selected Critical Prose*, ed. L. Dowling (New York: Penguin Classics, 1997), 10.

contemplative space where we can create something that we share with others.

Josef Pieper demonstrated to us the ontological condition of leisure as it relates to worship, the philosophical act, and God. What Pieper does not do is make explicitly clear the relationship between leisure and the communicative structure that organizes and propels our lives. Unearthing the relationship between leisure and communication provides a way for us to think about how we are to-be-in-the-world. Leisure provides us with an orientation to the world that is otherwise lost without the experience. Pieper gives us a nudge in the twentieth century that invites us to return to leisure for the sake of our sacred lives—he does this by arguing that leisure points us toward God. This book takes a communicative turn away from Pieper's trajectory. To make room for my own contribution to leisure and the human condition, I will provide a backdrop filtering through Pieper's push toward leisure and God and then turn toward leisure with a different approach, one that rethinks good and transcendence, though it is perhaps critical.

When we think of leisure today our impressions are drawn toward happiness, the good life, rest, relaxation of the mind and body, and to some extent, the freedom to be lazy.[2] In contemporary Western society the practice of leisure is often thought of as engaging recreative activities or refraining from activity. Part of this confusion is fueled by the all too popular linguistic label, *the leisure industry*, implying a *telos* related to production, consumption, and financial gain. In fact, as the discussion will come to reveal, the label, leisure industry, is oppositional to the inherent meaning of leisure in itself as the word *industry* implies a business activity or revenue. As a result of this confusion, which has been thrust upon us through economic and rhetorical manipulations, the contemporary understanding of leisure in society today has become synonymous with experiences of relaxation, rest, doing nothing, laziness, idleness, and in some cases, entertainment. I contend that whatever the gains of leisure we think might exist, the truth of leisure won't be experienced there. The aim of tending to leisure will always be

---

2   Not to negate the current literature on the needs for and effects of leisure,
     I invite you to consider some of the studies that inform our understanding
     of contemporary leisure and its implications to society (Winter 2002; Pais
     2006;Bowers 2007; Mannell 2007; Shaw 2007; Cushman and Gidlow
     2008; Edington 2006).

oblique—we will never quite be able to see where our leisure will take us, nevertheless, we must answer the call of leisure and remain open to impending possibilities. Tending to leisure is somewhat obstructed from our experience in the *leisure* industry in Western culture today. This book helps us to understand how we can better tend to leisure in our own lives despite the obliqueness that confronts us.

The leisure industry in American culture has matured with the pervasiveness of technology in our lives that propels the illusion of modernity through the metaphor of progress. Leisure has been lost in an instrumental scientific worldview and in order to recapture the spirit of leisure we must first realize that leisure is obscured from our vision. Public perception of leisure situates the action or activity of leisure into an external bodily action. There are two ways that leisure is talked about today, as recreation and as a therapy, but this does not get to the heart of leisure pointing back toward its philosophical origins. The problem with these two approaches to leisure, recreation and therapy, is that they begin with a presupposition as to the nature of leisure and that presupposition is incorrect. They do not fully articulate the importance of interiority to the action of leisure—in fact, the nature of leisure is often left unsaid. If they do articulate the nature of leisure, it often comes too late, perhaps as an afterthought. This is just the kind of approach to leisure that obscures it from us since leisure is at first an activity of the mind. I suggest that the need for wonder in our lives points to the same phenomenon, the ability to play and engage ideas in all of their potentialities, an activity that is generally obscured from contemporary society by the advancements in science and communicative technologies.

There is a sociological position related to leisure that emphasizes emotional intelligence and emotional labour.[3] Emotional intelligence involves basic grooming, exercise, cooking, reading newspapers, watching television, and listening to the radio, in the effort to increase one's emotional competency in their engagements with others. It is these qualities that cultivate personal confidence and people skills necessary for effective human communication. This means that the tools for cultivating one's mind comes from practicing leisure through external means more aptly described as informational repositories that sharpen one's emotional intelligence. In this way leisure and emotional

---

3   Christopher Rojek, *The Labour of Leisure* (Thousand Oaks, CA: Sage Publishing, 2010).

intelligence are counterparts. My study diverges from this perspective because it assumes an intentionality of a given action as a choice that one makes related to particular activities based upon how an individual judges her or his emotional intelligence. This kind of intentionality negates an aesthetic aspect of leisure in that the actor is intending to seek out a particular end while also considering consequences of one's choice, which sounds more like an act of goal-driven rationality than an action engaged in the aesthetic experience for the sake of the action itself.

Strict intentionality in the action of leisure is oppositional to an understanding of the Greek model of leisure which situates it as an action taken for the sake of the experience of the action itself. While this position is most certainly disagreeable today for some, it is helpful to understand leisure from a sociological framework as it does point us toward a relationship between leisure, work, labour, choice, freedom, and how we use our time. While we might have some similarities related to how we think about leisure, it is clear that a sociological perspective wants to measure data and privilege the external experience of leisure as opposed to the interior experience advocated in my philosophical approach.

When one is engaged in leisure one is not free in the colloquial sense, even though there is an engagement of free play that is constituted by moments of play that are open and unconstrained. In the leisure that I advocate in this project an intentional awareness is not permitted because that kind of focus enslaves us to a recreational *telos*. In this sense, recreational experiences teach us something sometimes but what we learn typically is not transformative and when it is, it is often short-lived. The outcomes, whether transformative or not, in leisure as a philosophical act (and not a sociological condition) are organic and have the greatest potential for transformative outcomes while not being presupposed or expected.

This purpose of this book is two-fold. First, it is an invitation to examine more fully the nature of leisure as a distinctly separate and perhaps a counterpart action to recreation. The second purpose of this book is to explore the nature of leisure from several different hermeneutic entrances driven by central metaphors that help to unfold the complex nature of leisure as a philosophical act and its impact to our communicative being. If we come to understand the experience of leisure as something separate and distinct from the experience of

recreation than we can shift our awareness toward something fundamentally necessary for the human communicative condition, a tending
to our communicative spirit that has social, phenomenological, ontological, and ethical implications. The heart of the philosophical act is
always already communication. We cannot embrace a more meaningful communicative spirit without understanding leisure in its multi-
fabricated philosophical aspects.

This project explores leisure as a philosophy of communication that
cultivates one's communicative self and community which enables authentic communicative engagement with the Other. I offer this careful
note about how this project has been organized. It is clear to me that
Calvin Schrag's relatively recent work is a helpful guide for me as I
think about the importance of leisure and philosophies of communication in relation to our communicative well-being. Therefore, I've
taken the liberty in the spirit of honoring his work to organize my in-
vestigation/reflections on leisure in a similar fashion as his 1997 publication, *The Self after Postmodernity*, by seeing it as Schrag saw the self
in discourse, in action, in community, and in transcendence. This will
offer a constructive way to think about leisure philosophically while
embedded within our historical moment. Exploring leisure in this
way helps us to situate the *tending to* leisure after postmodernity in a
way that makes sense to us. The following chapter overviews provide a
glimpse into that framework.

CHAPTER OVERVIEWS

Chapter 1, *Transformative Leisure in Discourse*, explores the nature of
transformative leisure through narrative and historicity. A rationale
for revisiting the concept of leisure philosophically reveals a significance and inherent value to the human condition. This project is responding to questions within our particular historical moment that
unfold within a *calming drama* that has disrupted the routine of daily
toil. A calming drama disrupts what this project has come to describe
as an atrophic way of thinking about and doing leisure. An atrophic
condition celebrates no distinction between leisure and recreation and
this condition alone permits and encourages the routine to remain
routine. Thus, the atrophy of leisure becomes a history which is no
longer responsive to contemporary stimuli. This chapter explores the
public discourse of leisure and forges three metaphysical conditions
situated on a continuum that provides textured examples delineating

transformative leisure from recreation. This chapter also includes a discussion of the value of leisure as a philosophy of communication and its significance to the communicative turn.

Chapter 2, *Transformative Leisure in Action*, considers the phenomenological experience of the "making" or "doing" of leisure. This chapter explores transformative leisure in lived action by considering the phenomenological experience that is at once tied to ethics in action related to self and other. The importance of a phenomenological consideration of leisure begins with the idea that presence and absence co-exist in the engagement of transformative leisure and acknowledging that without this co-existence in the *doing* of transformative leisure there is an incompleteness that consequently creates a false consciousness. The idea of being present does not simply mean being somewhere with something else at the same time but it means more so to be present in participation or in action with something else. To understand something does not necessarily mean to reason or come to judgment after identifying a logically well-reasoned assertion. Rather it means to have a present involvement in the idea that is being said. This is not a relationship (in the adjectival sense) between persons or between a reader and an author but it is a sharing (in the verb sense) in what the text (written or spoken) shares with us. These are the phenomenological aspects of transformative leisure in action that help to reveal the essence of the experience itself.

Chapter 3, *Transformative Leisure in Community*, considers transformative leisure through an ontological and existential lens that considers both realms of public and private communicative action. This experience is embedded within a particular socioeconomic reality that provides for difference and otherness to remain a core consideration of how we ought to respond. By reaching out for insight from Karl Marx's philosophy on the metaphor of alienation, aspects of transformative leisure are situated within socioeconomic conditions that confront communicative agents on a daily basis. Metaphors of alienation, consumption, production, and exploitation threaten the virtuous community and lead us toward recreative fetishism, which is representative of how contemporary society engages leisure (or what they think is leisure). But Marx's philosophy is incomplete to consider fully leisure therefore, Hannah Arendt's work redirects the assumptions of Marx by redefining concepts like work, action, and labour, as well as realms of engagement, most notably, her identification of the social realm. This chapter provokes a phenomenological alternative for engagement in the world with otherness through an individual's understanding and commitment to transformative leisure.

Transformative leisure is identified as having inherent political qualities or potential as Arendt calls for a correction of past political and social mistakes by embracing *phronesis* and *praxis* in lived public action. In this corrective space, the interspaces within the public realm have the potential to embrace human plurality and create a vibrant public domain of human participants. This new space would be able to reach between the hearts of people and their ideologies in the spirit of respect. There would be no dictating any particular social or political way of engagement. However, what Arendt saw in these new public political interspaces was a dangerous political domain imbued with the illusionary aspects of liberation and political action. Arendt referred to leisure in the spirit of the contemplative life as a way of preparing for one to engage in a plurality-imbued public sphere. Because of this contemplative spirit we can begin to engage ideas more deeply and constructively. Arendt wants people to not only think philosophically and thoughtfully, but to also act upon those thoughts in an engagement with efficacy and authenticity toward ideas and toward others. This reality is not in response to a theoretical dictum but it is out of the acknowledgement of the trace of the face of the other that is always already nudging us to respond and engage with the other.

Chapter 4, *Transformative Leisure in Transcendence,* moves us forward in a *tending-to* something that is vital for human communicative engagement. Understanding transformative leisure in transcendence moves us beyond discourse, action, and community in a way that acknowledges the ethicality of such beingness. This chapter specifically considers the ethical philosophies of Emanuel Levinas and Josepf Pieper who enter the conversation from two very different ethical perspectives. Alterity confronts us in a way that invites us to think about how we live with others in a responsive space beyond the individual self and other. Emanuel Levinas articulates his ethical philosophy via the notion of alterity as the other holds us in demand, not so much the person, but it is the trace or echo of the other that holds us in an ethical *apriori* condition.[4] Leisure provides us one way to attend to the revelatory call from the other that which holds us in demand and creates an

---

4   Emmanuel Levinas, *Totality and Infinity: An Essay on Exteriority,* trans. A. Lingis (Pittsburgh, PA: Duquesne University Press., 2000).

existential rupture of our agency. If we do not attend to that demand we turn away from the other causing an existential disruption, much like a recreative condition that replaces our experience of leisure. As we move toward that demand, we seek to respond fittingly within the particularity of the context and narrative in which we find ourselves. Our responsibility to the other transcends individual boundaries as we co-construct a communicative environment of infinite possibilities. Acknowledging that there are a multiplicity of communication ethics perspectives, I've also chosen to articulate transformative leisure as a virtue ethic by making a conscious effort to situate my argument within the framework of Josef Pieper's virtue ethic philosophy and argue that transformative leisure cultivates a virtue ethic of Being.

It is hardly appropriate to talk about communication action or any other kinds of action without the acknowledgment of ethics in some way. This chapter explicitly ties ethics and transcendence together as it illuminates the realities inherent in transformative leisure. Unlike recreation that has no long-lasting implications to the self, leisure has transformative power that opens the self to possibilities toward transcendence. Transcendence culminates from an attunement of the self that moves one to action in such a way that tends to community and the other; transcendence liberates the communicative being through a narratival responsiveness within a praxial spirit that gives life to the self and to others.

Chapter 5, *Conclusion: Tending to Transformative Leisure*, provides a synthesis of the previous chapters and returns to the work of Calvin Schrag to help us grasp the value of a life imbued with transformative leisure. This chapter weaves together a picture of transcendence of the self through leisure by tending to Calvin Schrag's semantic experiment in *The Self after Postmodernity* and Pierre Hadot's reflections on spiritual exercises from *Philosophy as a Way of Life*. This last chapter is a call to our conscience, asking us if we have identified how we, in our own lives, experience leisure and how do we ensure that we have both leisure and recreation in our lives for health of our interiority. This chapter reaffirms what is at stake here—and it is more than our actions, it is the life of our mind. We begin with our illumination of transformative leisure through a consideration of leisure and in discourse in order to lay forth our path of discovery.

CHAPTER I

TRANSFORMATIVE LEISURE IN DISCOURSE

Leisure, then, as a condition of the soul – (and we must firmly keep to this assumption, since leisure is not necessarily in all the external things like "breaks," "time off," "weekend," "vacation," and so on – it is a condition of the soul) – leisure is precisely the counterpoise to the image of the "worker."

– Josef Pieper

philosophy as a voice in the conversation of humankind needs to remain conversant with preceding voices, and this remains a requirement in any explication of the role of the fitting response... [t]he communicative turn in its move beyond metaphysics, encounters the demand for a cultural hermeneutics to sort out the meaning of our historical inherence.

– Calvin O. Schrag

Ontological hermeneutics point us toward a linguisticality of being that constitutes the self through lived speech acts. This creates a dynamics of narrative in which the self is implicated through lived communicative action with and among others. The horizon of possibilities of meaning in this dynamic narratival space is infinite. This means that narratives play a constitutive role in the discourse of the self. It is in this sense that discourse is used in this project. The self begins with the other in discourse and that beginning is dynamic, contextual, and both public and private. Narratives are also explanatory devices that shape how we experience the other within contexts. Therefore, narratives bring epistemological and hermeneutical clarity to how we experience the world around us.[1] Since the self emerges out of the narratives we experience, it is helpful to explore the self in relation to transformative leisure in discourse. Therefore, this chapter first explores leisure in discourse governed by a selected and historically situated narrative. Second, a deliberate discussion distinguishing transformative leisure from recreation through metaphors situated upon a continuum of discovery leads toward the third and final part of this chapter. In this final section, a consideration of transformative leisure through the lens of historicity helps to illuminate the questions that undergird this project. So now, I begin with a look at the discourse of transformative leisure.

A DISCOURSE OF TRANSFORMATIVE LEISURE: NOT RECREATION

The most obvious difference between transformative leisure and recreation is the action of contemplation—transformative leisure has it and recreation does not. Contemplation is the heart of the transformative value that transformative leisure potentially provides because it is through contemplation that the soul or interiority becomes elevated. It is in this kind of activity of the mind that transformative leisure opens the communicative being to the "whole of time and being" which elevates the soul beyond the mundane world.[2] This means that it is through transformative leisure that one's ontological, phenomenological, existential, and philosophical act permits one's interiority to be wholly experienced and consummated in such a way that we can be transformed—or at least the potential is there. To say that if one engages in transformative leisure then one *will* be transformed is an inaccurate statement because it presupposes an expectation and places a demand upon the particular action. Transformative leisure does not entail any expectation and or demand from the engagement. Therefore, it is more accurate to say there is a potential for transformation of some kind when one practices transformative leisure.

This is a radical revisioning of a concept that has been the topic of philosophical discussions at least since early Greek civilization. Plato's

---

1   Calvin O. Schrag, *The Self After Postmodernity* (New Haven, CT: Yale University Press, 1997).

2   Pierre Hadot, *What is Ancient Philosophy?* (Cambridge, MA: Belknap Harvard University Press, 2004), 203.

allegory of the cave points to the value and virtue of transformative leisure. In *The Republic*, Plato suggested that in order to really understand one's environment, one must turn away from their daily toil, their "fetters and their folly" in order to see the reality of their existence.[3] This kind of turning away from what we know is difficult since it is more comfortable to remain in one's ignorance than to venture out into the unknown. For Plato, this turning away would be a turning toward divine contemplations where one is awakened and learns new things about their own reality and existence. However, as Plato advocated, once one turns away from their daily follies, one must then turn back toward those still entwined in that ignorance and help them to see the truth in order to free them. So in order to be effective within our mortal coil we must first turn away from it. Divine turning is a reflexive activity where one is removed from her or his daily toil.

This kind of philosophical life becomes a life habituated in transformative leisure and this habituation prevents one from becoming a slave to one's desires and pleasures that have no meaning to our higher selves. Plato tied the active political life to a life of transformative leisure in that he suggested the best ruler (who turns out to be the philosopher king) is the ruler who is not driven by expedient pursuits or agency. The philosopher, one who loves wisdom, habituates a contemplative life which cultivates a communicative spirit that acknowledges community and collective justice. Of course, not all philosophers agreed with Plato.

Aristotle situated leisure as an ethical part of one's life in Book X of *The Nicomachean Ethics* when he stated that one's happiness depends on leisure because the activity is contemplative and engaged for its own sake, since nothing material actually arises from the activity. What this means is that nothing of substance actually emerges except for happiness in one's being. As Aristotle continued to tease out aspects of this kind of contemplative action, he suggested that contemplative leisure is a virtuous activity that becomes linked to practical wisdom, *phronesis*. So, we can understand that leisure is not only connected to the passions of our contemplative spirit but also is then linked to practical wisdom. Additionally, practical wisdom is interconnected with excellence in reasoning, which is considered an intellectual virtue. This is important in that transformative leisure gives us something to share

3   Plato, *The Republic*, trans. E. H. Warmington and P. G. Rouse (New York: Signet Classics, 1984), 313; 516B.

with others—conversational attributes that enable us to constructively communicate with others in ways that do not lead toward negative phatic styles of communication. Transformative leisure gives us something to talk about with others that is not deemed hurtful or binding in any way.

When we have something constructive to say, even in contentious environments, we communicatively engage in an ethical space that honors the other in a way that demonstrates a gentle spirit undergirded by intellectual generosity. Being that transformative leisure begins contemplatively and quietly, we can see how one's practical and intellectual virtues are shaped through this kind of productive silence. In silence, the intellectual productivity manifests in active thought and ultimately in one's deed. Aristotle provided a rationale for recognizing a distinction between transformative leisure and recreation because he acknowledged that one cannot get to virtue through amusement or recreation—the path to virtue comes through a habit of transformative leisure. In fact the contemplative life offers the highest potential toward the attainment of happiness. Happiness depends on transformative leisure and it (leisure) is the first principle of all action.[4] This first principle positions transformative leisure as an *apriori* condition that we ought to recognize and embrace. It is a condition that gives us communicative life.

Today the statement that leisure and recreation are two very different experiences is not generally accepted unless one is familiar with the classical origins of leisure. Furthermore, most people are resistant to the idea that leisure (and not recreation) can recuperate, repair, and rejuvenate one's communicative spirit. The reason for this lack of awareness can be attributed to a public eclipse of the understanding of the philosophical nature of leisure and its distinction from recreation[5].

Thorstein Veblen's (1899/1953) economic theory included a critique of the leisure class who he described as people moving from one mindless activity to another for the purpose of showing off to others as the activity provided a prestigious or elevated social/economic status of the actors. Veblen propelled the philosophical confusion between

---

4   Aristotle, *Politics*, trans. R. McKeon (New York: Modern Library, 2001b).

5   The distinction between transformative leisure and recreation is more fully articulated in my earlier work, 2007. *Transformative leisure: Recuperative Praxis for Human Communication. Milwaukee, WI*: Marquette University Press.

leisure and recreation because he was critiquing a way of life created by a mechanistic framework and the modern industrial revolution
that liberated people from their work experience. What Veblen actually critiqued was a conspicuous engagement of recreation. However,
he did refer to these kinds of actions as a practice of *conspicuous consumption* and *pecuniary emulation*—or more notably, a public fraud.
In retrospect, Veblen emerges as offering a prophetic warning about
what he could foresee as widespread problems in a society constituted
by the massification of the quick and the fast. Today, his critique of the
leisure class leads us back toward the Greek ideal of transformative leisure. Ancient philosophers saw leisure as hard work, reflective engagement, and a contemplative action, but somewhere in public thought
and practices, the contemplative and philosophical understanding of
leisure was displaced.

Thorstein Veblen had a deconstructive view on the usage and mis-
usage of things and money by the human agent. In particular, there
is a distinction between activities that are productive and useful and
those that are ostentatious. Consistent with the environment that
Veblen critiqued, today labour has become irksome to some people
who would rather increase their property ownership, retire at age for-
ty, and not have to work for a living. This critique of the leisure class
resonates with the idea of a business enterprise when people become
wasteful as they flaunt their engagement of needless activities which
demonstrate an excessive waste in time and accumulation of things
that they want but that they do not need. Veblen went so far as to say
that human beings believed that money is not good unless you flaunt
it, waste it, and show it off to others. In many ways, the industrial era
carved out an understanding of leisure that had became more connected to hedonism than to intellectual virtue and interior cultivation
of the communicative being. Today transformative leisure is simply
synonymous with recreation.

The connection of transformative leisure to the idea of production
and consumption more fully obscured leisure from its original philosophical and contemplative framework. Growing public discourse
on leisure (without philosophy or an *aleisure* experience) and its increased economic value is part of the discourse that amplified and
strengthened the eclipse of leisure. Consequently, public discourse
that emerged out of the industrial era also contributed to the development of the leisure industry as we know it today as well as the idea

that leisure has now become a commodity. In this sense, leisure as an industry helps to blur and maintain the distinction between transformative leisure and recreation. So, the task now is to explicate the nature of recreation and then offer three sets of metaphors to texture our understanding so that a clear distinction is made between the two concepts and actions.

Recreation is an activity people do that interrupts daily mundane tasks, including work at the office or at home. The idea behind recreation is somewhat like taking a coffee break while at work. Recreation permits people to take a break from their business and busy-ness of everyday tasks in order to do something different. This is a necessary component of our daily lives––but it is not transformative leisure. Transformative leisure is hard work and the key to doing it is in the approach we take to a particular action, which should be in the spirit of serious play, or *poiesis*—that is, a creative making of something. The mindful attention you give the activity is what makes the difference between transformative leisure and recreation. But there are other differences too.

Leisure and recreation have very different assumptions, methods, *telos*, and temporality associated with them, however, both leisure and recreation are needed to cultivate and satisfy human experiences. Recreation is approached epistemologically since it relies upon the acquisition of knowledge to be able to recreate. For example: If I want to play baseball I need to learn the rules, perhaps learn about protective gear, and nonverbal signals in order to play the game with others. If I stop at gaining knowledge, I am likely recreating; if I want to win a game or the championship, the experience is also recreation. This kind of focus of intention to play the game is connected to a *telos* driven by competition—or at the very least, some kind of particular outcome. On the other hand, transformative leisure has an ontological and phenomenological orientation. I play the violin and I attend to the notes, the musical syntax, and the authorial intent of a piece. I consider the voice and its relation to the potential other voices involved in the piece (assuming I am playing a musical composition that is written for violin and at least one other instrument). I play my violin and I experience the music. I am not concerned with the end of the piece because my focus resides within the experience of the piece. The music becomes my ground from which I make decisions about articulations and bowings. In this play of transformative leisure I am making something and

I exist within that something as it emerges and co-creates the experience with me. The music is born and it continues to be born as I, through my agency, become lost in the play. Sometimes we talk about this as "being in the moment" which means that my focus is on the play itself and not on the outcome of the moment. In fact, phenomena outside of that experience do not exist to me in my moments of play. In some way, as I engage in this kind of play, my experience of space and time alters or changes from the mundane to the transcendent.

On the other hand, the method of recreation begins with the acquisition of knowledge and ultimately leads to the performance of an activity that has a social value. In a recreational activity, the focus is generally on the social aspect or the end result, not on the play itself. Whether children/youth soccer leagues or adult softball leagues, recreation leads us somewhere through a linear model governed by a set of rules that might end with a tournament title or a trophy but the key difference is the focus of attention which is centered upon the end result. This differs from the approach to transformative leisure where the phenomenological focus of attention is on the play itself, which privileges the interplay and cointending of presence and absence within the particular experience and not on the social aspect or the outcome. *Telos* in recreation is connected to the notion of progress and the linear completion of an activity. *Telos* in leisure is connected to-the-thing-itself, an experience engulfed within the action, contemplative or physical, as a movement without a beginning and without an end.

Finally, as suggested earlier, time is experienced much differently in the "doing of" recreation and transformative leisure. Time in recreation is based on *chronos*, chronological movement toward a time or a level that demarcates the end of some thing. Chronos is typically connected with regular everyday rhythms of our everyday life. Chronos is connected to a natural time; chronos is our experience governed by the natural world.[6] Chronos governs when we wake, sleep, eat, and keep daily appointments. Chronos depends upon the sun, the stars, and the moon. Chronos measures our day for us and dictates our work, holidays, and basic governance of our country. Chronos is both individual and communal.

---

6   Charles Guignon, K. Aho, "Phenomenological Reflections on Work and Leisure in America," in *The Value of Time and Leisure in a World of Work*, ed. M. R. Haney and A. David Kline (Lanham, MD: Lexington Books, 2010), 25-38.

Time in transformative leisure is experienced more as temporality and becomes intertwined with our Being. In transformative leisure time is ontologically eternal and disconnected from any sense of *chronos* as it can be considered "a time outside of time".[7] This means that the experience is situated within an intellectual knowing of the opportune time or more specifically, a kairotic moment or moments of time. In Greek mythology, *Kairos* was the youngest son of Zeus and typically personified as Opportunity.[8] The stories of *Kairos* have contributed to our understanding of *kairos* denoting a sense of timeliness or doing something that feels particularly appropriate at the right moment. Not only does *kairos* point to a timeliness of an action but it also points to a particular transforming moment such as the resurrection of Christ, the election of the first African American President in the United States, or the horrific events on September 11, 2001 in the United States that touched many other nations around the world. This sense of time is not confined within the limits of the natural world. *Kairos* points to a time beyond measured time; it is time within experience governed only by the experience itself, which implies it is ungoverned and unmeasured by external preconditions. This is a moment that is both outside of time and higher than time.[9] These kinds of moments liberate us from daily toils and invite us to see the possibilities in communicative environments.

When I play my violin time does not pass chronologically. In my experience, rather in my playing, I engage and re-engage my instrument and my notes while not attending to worldly time and not attending to ending a passage. I play within an ontological presence until I am exhausted physically and I have lost myself in that play. In transformative leisure, temporality is not measured, instead, it is experienced.

In a more provocative approach to illuminate the difference between transformative leisure and recreation we can use a continuum to consider metaphors that situate the differences between transformative leisure and recreation within approach, action, and outcome. When thinking about transformative leisure and recreation oppositionally, there three are metaphorical pairs that come to mind; they are,

---

7   Guignon and Aho, "Phenomenological Reflections," 30.

8   Christopher L. Johnstone, *Listening to the Logos: Speech and the Coming of Wisdom in Ancient Greece* (Columbia, SC: University of South Carolina Press, 2009).

9   Guignon and Aho, "Phenomenological Reflections."

craftsmen/technicians (related to the artfulness of the approach), participants/spectators (related to the action), and play/game (related to the intentionality and outcome). It is important to see these pairings on a continuum that shift and change moment to moment. It is also important to acknowledge that these pairings are not fixed in time and space but they are placed freely on a continuum that responds to moments in a kairotic and spatial framework. The first metaphorical pair is craftsmen/technicians.

CRAFTSMEN-TECHNICIANS

By starting with this particular metaphorical pairing I am focusing on the artfulness of the experience. My intention is to not dismiss either one of them; nor is it my intention to create a hierarchy. Instead, the metaphorical pairing helps us to see a qualitative difference between two kinds of engagement. Craftsmen (not intended to gender the activity) attend to their craft in a way that differs from technicians. The craftsman is demarcated as one that experiences the activity beyond acknowledging the rules and regulations; beyond what a technical expert might know or do.[10] Anyone can learn the rules, understand the process/procedure, and recall tedious information that is only useful now and then and this is what the technician does. The technician has knowledge that is connected to varying levels of experience but many expert technicians do not like what they do. Often, these kinds of expert technicians are engaged in the activity for monetary compensation, for reasons related to a lack of having nothing better to do or having no other options/opportunities, or simply because the person has settled into a routine—in any case, these technicians do not love their craft. The craftsman loves the craft.

The craftsman is one who brings skill, commitment, and judgment to the experience in a way that does not surrender to emotivism.[11] An expert technician will know how to handle intricate challenges of the craft, though not necessarily appreciate the challenges—and in fact, might even resent or regret those challenges. On the other hand, the craftsman loves those challenges inherent in the craft, in fact he or

---

10   Aristotle, *Nicomachean Ethics*, (Oxford: Oxford University Press, 1998).
11   Richard Sennett, *Fall of Public Man*, (New York: W. W. Norton & Company, 1974).

she might even thrive on those challenges. The technician seeks out
the most practical step ín an activity, though it might not be the *right*
thing to do—perhaps it is the easiest or least expensive way of doing
things.[12]

As we think of these slight differences between the craftsman/tech-
nician approach to experience related to transformative leisure, coming
to terms with Arendt's notion of labour is helpful because labour, that
activity, which is necessary to sustain life, is what a craftsman seeks. A
technician seeks to do work for money or for résumé building, but not
for the love of the experience itself. It is love for the experience that
sustains our spiritual lives and makes our physical lives much healthier. The action of transformative leisure is akin to the action of a craftsman. In the spirit of transformative leisure we embrace the experience
from a contemplative starting place that engages the challenges that
wholly emerge within given experiences. The love of the craft (or for
the craft), whether situated within playing music, learning to ice skate,
bowling, or building kitchen cabinets resides in the heart of the experience and the activity for the sake of itself. This love is cultivated and
contemplated within the individual until the action emerges. Having
an intended outcome would shift this activity toward a different and
opposing end, rendering it to be recreation—not transformative leisure. Simply put, a craftsman is to transformative leisure as a technician is to recreation. Recreation might (though not always) require an
expertise but the experience is not driven by the activity or the love of
the activity, rather it is driven by external conditions or preferences.
Considering intentionality as a condition that provides insight to the
qualitative difference between transformative leisure and recreation is
a starting place for us. The next set of metaphor pairs, participant and
spectator, help us to understand this distinction through action.

PARTICIPANTS-SPECTATORS

The public domain is at risk of falling into a fractured communicative space where human beings to take communicative action which
ultimately is what creates and shapes the public domain.[13] People not
only will *not* act, they will not be *aware* that they do not act, or at

12   Ronald C. Arnett, "Leisure and the Communicative Praxis of Craft,"
     Listening: Journal of Communication Ethics, Religion, and Culture 46, no. 1
     (2011): 21-36.
13   Sennett, *Fall of Public Man.*

least they will be indifferent to the need for a publicly engaged action. A spectator watches and perhaps comes to a judgment based upon observation, not experience. Spectatorship is dangerous because one makes assumptions and judgments that are separate from action or experience and it can encourage complacency and laziness. Sometimes it is all right to be a spectator but a life lived as a spectator renders a human agent empty and enslaved to the will and power of others as well as to society as a whole. There are times we can and should be a spectator, especially when public politeness and decorum are required (such as listening to a public presidential debate). But there are other times when the circumstances require or demand a response, in particular a fitting response. It is in each of these moments that spectatorship is insufficient and for some, unethical.

Being a participant requires action, acknowledgment, and a consciousness that extends beyond the self. Participants have the ability to move beyond emotivism and to see things otherwise. Being a spectator does not mean that one merely does not act. A spectator can sit idle or act without being informed. For example, in transformative leisure a communicative participant begins an activity from a contemplative spirit which can potentially lead to the communicant physically acting in some way. This could range from thinking about an instrument (i.e. how it should be in tune or what kind of scale one wants to play...and what that means in regards to intervals, articulations, tempos, and dynamics) to the actual physical playing of scales. Though, the communicative participant does not need to actually play the instrument for this experience to be transformative leisure. An example of this would involve an individual who loves the craft of music but doesn't actually play an instrument, yet is ever so active in the contemplative aspect of music and this contemplative spirit moves the communicative participant to become a subscriber to an orchestra, band, or theatre group. Transformative leisure would be exemplified by the contemplative beginnings of *attention* in listening to and learning about the particular music involved. It would then continue in the communicative participant's interactions and discussions with others who might share the same interest or perhaps have other related interests. This communicative participant enjoys the challenges in listening to different kinds of music, attending live shows, supporting the arts in other ways and so forth. The communicative participant is actively engaged somehow that enables continued learning even without learning the instrument.

In a similar way, everyone who acts is not acting as a participant and is therefore, not engaging transformative leisure. In fact, this is the most obvious juncture where the distinction between transformative leisure and recreation manifests. A person acting not from a contemplative spirit but perhaps from a competitive spirit that limits the experience is one who exemplifies the notion of spectator. A spectator either does not act, acts without being informed, or simply acts from a predetermine *telos* that is often imposed upon by others. The philosophically free spirit of contemplation does not exist in spectatorship. So, if someone acts because of someone else or in the spirit of another, or acts in the spirit of Veblen's pecuniary emulation or conspicuous consumption, the actor misses the fruitful potential that is inherent in the transformative potentiality of transformative leisure and can be limited to that of spectator status indeterminately. For many, that status is acceptable. Now, *spectator* is not a bad word nor is it a bad action. The status of spectator is simply different from the status of participant. To further explicate this distinction between transformative leisure and recreation, a discussion of the nature of the action related to intentionality and outcome is helpful and this is exemplified through the juxtaposition of play and game and a focus on intentionality related to outcome.

PLAY-GAME

To clarify, this is not a discussion of game theory which has found a growing home in the communication discipline. Rather, when the term play is posited, I refer to the notion of *poiesis*, as a creative making that is forged from a person's hand or the hand of nature.[14] There is a mindful shaping of a thing that comes to life from the crafting together by the creator's metaphorical hand. This metaphorical hand includes the mind, the active interiority that has had some time in contemplating this thing itself. Contemplation is a processual engagement because it does not have an end rather it continues and emerges. It is a poetic play that creates something otherwise. Intentionality is focused inwardly, not toward an external outcome.

When one engages or interacts in a game with her or himself or others, intentionality is often driven by the rules of the game and the

---

14   Pat Arneson, *Perspectives on Philosophy of Communication*, (West Lafayette, IN: Purdue University Press, 2007).

past practices of the players. The engagement becomes scripted and often nothing new happens other than from the element of chance like throwing dice (in a board game) or wind (in a baseball game). The players want to "win" rather than experience the throw of the die or connect the bat to the ball for the sake of the experience. Games are generally driven by rules and procedures. They are carefully scripted and mathematically generated. Games are recreative and fun but they will not transform one's interiority. Games can keep us healthy and fit. Games can provide us with exercise to keep us physically flexible. Games can refresh our minds ever so briefly during a hectic day but these outcomes have only temporal implications. Eventually you will become tired, sore, and weak again. The potential outcome of leisure is not temporal in this sense. The transformative potential in leisure is situated in the serendipitous experience of attending to-the-thing-itself in such a way that is not driven by external factors like game rules and other constraints. The idea of play is that it is unrestrained and uninhibited by competition, emotivism, pressure from others, or confined within a one dimensional playground. Play is open and invitational. When one plays, one does not look at the time or think about the end. There is no end in play unlike a game where the end comes with a winner. Winning does not affect play. Play is. Play becomes. Play has a phenomenological presence that is inescapably different from game. Sometimes the experience of play and game can overlap or blend together and between depending upon one's phenomenological focus of attention at any given moment.

VALUE OF THE CONTINUUM

Understanding these definitional distinctions does not negate or destroy leisure or recreation. Instead, this is helpful to understand our human needs and actions as they phenomenologically exist. Human beings need both kinds of activities in our lives. Unfortunately, today in our fast-paced mediated environment we often forget the slower of the two activities. Since leisure begins from a contemplative spirit, it does not attract our attention because of its slowness. But the value of leisure is inherently in its slowness.[15] The idea of slow is something we no longer tolerate in our society because the pervasiveness of media

15   Mitchell R. Haney, "The Value of Slow," in *The Value of Time and Leisure in a World of Work*, ed. M. R. Haney and A. David Kline (Lanham, MD: Lexington Books, 2010), 151-164.

has trained us, as spectators, to accept that everything should be in the here and now, not in the *to be* or *not yet*. We have difficulty slowing down. The idea of slow enables the play that is necessary for the contemplative spirit. It is easy to recreate because media train or enslave spectators. There is less risk (if any) and places to hide in spectatorship. To play as a participant, we put ourselves *out there* to learn, explore, and experience things outside of our control. Control sets limits and in play, there are no limits. Sifting through these metaphorical parings, a distinction between transformative leisure and recreation has emerged that hopefully clarifies what I mean as I advocate a return to the authentic notion of leisure, philosophically.

Finally, I gather my thoughts bringing clarity to the distinction between transformative leisure and recreation, which is that transformative leisure constitutes a good life, a virtuous life, the foundation of human culture, and it is necessary nourishment for the human soul/ interiority. Recreation cannot provide that kind of interior cultivation because recreation is an external experience which does not privilege or emphasize contemplation or *poiesis* within our interiority. In leisure there is a becoming, a transformation, a catharsis that is not intended, yet it occurs, somewhere, somehow, without provocation other than the play itself. This means that the transformation cannot be intended rather it is an organic experience that is unique and serendipitous. It cannot be re-experienced, it simply is. Recognizing this distinction between transformative leisure and recreation is one way to illuminate the hidden or eclipsed value of a life practiced with leisure.

Exploring the differences between transformative leisure and recreation opens this study with clear and distinct guidelines for understanding the nature of two kinds of activities, as well as the pragmatic applications of them. My journey inside transformative leisure acknowledges the relevance of Calvin Schrag's philosophy of communication as he considers the self in discourse, action, community, and transcendence. My approach secularizes Pieper's perspective of leisure as a way to God. My divergence from Pieper explores transformative leisure in discourse, transformative leisure in action, transformative leisure in community, and transformative leisure in transcendence as a way to conceptualize and embody transformative leisure after or beyond a postmodern context that acknowledges our contentious yet serendipitous historical moment. The idea of *tending* to leisure is critical to the human condition. *Tending* to leisure in our lives begins within a contemplative spirit but does not stop there. Leisure does not separate one from the world instead, it prepares us to be active and ethical agents in the world as we live with and among others.

TRANSFORMATIVE LEISURE AND HISTORICITY

A descriptive discussion of transformative leisure enables one to observe or count the differences between leisure and recreation in an applied context. In order to unfold the multi-textured nature of the problem of transformative leisure today, an examination of leisure phenomenologically is helpful and can provide a more thorough and comprehensive understanding of its value to the human experience and condition. This chapter uses historicity to discuss the phenomenological aspects of transformative leisure and identifies how this particular project is responding to a question in a given historical moment that unfolds an unassuming tension. The unassuming tension is a disruption of the routine and perhaps an awakening of an impairment of the way people think and do transformative leisure.

There is an atrophy of our leisure consciousness when one fails to celebrate the distinction between transformative leisure and recreation. This failure permits and encourages the routine to remain routine. Thus, the atrophy of leisure becomes a history situated outside of historicity in which it is no longer responsive to the world around it. The condition of atrophy becomes a 'telling' or a "said" of a story.[16] In contrast, it is the act of *saying* with which this project is concerned. There are three main aspects related to transformative leisure and the communicative being that begin this part of our journey. The first aspect is the idea of historicity as opposed to history. The second aspect is about identifying the question(s) in a given historical moment, which is a central point for historicity and in doing so, the questions that drive this study are illuminated. The third aspect is a kind of rationale for using different hermeneutic entrances to explore transformative leisure phenomenologically. The central thread for each of these sections resides within the notion of historicity.

Historicity is alive and immediate. History tells a story about something said but historicity is more complex and dynamic than a fixed or static notion of that something. Hans Georg Gadamer suggested that:

---

16   Levinas, *Entre Nous*, 63.

[t]here is something immediately evident about grounding philosophical and historical studies and the ways the human sciences
work on this concept of the sensus communis. For their object, the
moral and historical existence of humanity, as it takes shape in our
words and deeds, is itself decisively determined by the sensus communis. Thus a conclusion based on universals, a reasoned proof, is
not sufficient, because what is decisive is the circumstances.[17]

Practical wisdom (*phronesis*) situated within the immediacy of
experience often, or more often, prevails over a well-reasoned proof.
Gadamer suggested that the moral element that ensures the primacy
of sensus communis is the immediacy of it, or the idea that its focus
remains in the present day moment. So, the currency of the questions
of any given historical moment is what defines sensus communis, or
historicity, as opposed to the notion of history that which is static and
unchangeable.

The telling of a story has no life as it just "is" or "was" and there is no
longer a "doing" or a *poiesis* connected to it. A telling keeps the distinction between transformative leisure and recreation irrelevant and situated within the static boundary of history. This project responds to
the calling out, the revelatory call or echo that which is a quiet drama.
Leisure has lost its meaning in contemporary society and has become
at one with recreation. Questions that face us today pertaining to our
existential angst include: how does one turn toward a more productive life without losing one's self to everyday toil and what is it about
current notions of leisure that misleads humanity into thinking that
they are being recuperated through their leisure activity, when most
of us adhere to the adage, "I need a vacation from my vacation"? These
questions call out to those who listen to the public discourse about
leisure and invite us back into a philosophical understanding of leisure
and a true recuperative experience; this is the quiet drama of the call.
It is a revelatory call and our responsibility, to hear it and then to do
something about it.

Common sense is a necessary and essential aspect of a humanistic
tradition and the cultivation of a sense of community, referred to as
sensus communis.[18] Giovanni Battista Vico's (1668-1744) sense of wis-

---

17   Gadamer, *Truth and Method*, 22-23.
18   Giovanni Battista Vico, *On the Study Methods of Our Time*, trans. E.
Gianturco (Indianapolis, IN: Bobbs-Merrill Publishing, 1965).

dom comes out of the Humanistic tradition that focused on the notion of speaking well or *eu legein*. So, to not only know what to say but to know how to say it is an essential skill. *Sensus communis* is essential to the notion of historicity as it points to the questions that temporally call out to given historical moments. In our contemporary age, the questions that we encounter have some form of commonality situated within similar interests in the reality of every day engagement between human interlocutors.[19] In the spirit of this project, the *sensus communis* has already experienced the public fraud in the lack of understanding between the two concepts, leisure and recreation. People already know that they are tired, addicted to technologies that remove them from human engagement, and have an insatiable desire for things at any cost. Historicity permits us to hear this revelatory call and invites us to attempt to look for responses that are fitting and appropriate. In this framework, one needs a hermeneutic humility that listens for these calls and guides one's path in seeking a fitting response.

In our attempt to look for a fitting response or responses, agreement on the question makes developing public discourse about the question possible. Because of this, historicity becomes a communicative call that announces itself within the human experience and between human interlocutors that demands our attention and provides us no alternative. An example of this involves recognizing the multiplicity of responses to a particular historical question that which differentiates one communicative position from another. In this current historical moment we see, on a daily basis, war and death pervade daily life in the Middle East because there are different responses to age old questions of religious freedom, gender equality, and experiences of personal security shape the pragmatic communicative interactions of individuals and interlocutors each day.[20]

Historicity is not relative and questions do not change at the whim of individuals. Historicity involves multiple factors and complexities that are really outside of the power of the communicative agent. An important aspect of historicity is that it is the nature of the question that is important and not individual preferences or influence. Historicity requires a diligent communicator to listen carefully and hear those

---

19   Ronald C. Arnett, P. Arneson, A. M. Holba, "Bridges Not Walls: The Communicative Enactment of Dialogic Storytelling," Review of Communication 8, no. 3 (2008): 217-234.

20   Ibid.

common sense questions that call out in a given historical moment. This kind of listening must occur by standing within the moment and not from a place of judgment outside of the particular moment. If one listens carefully, similar questions might emerge at different times throughout history, which can link two moments in history together with a common set of questions. So, while, historically (as we might see in a history book) the temporal elements might be disparate, their temporality is joined together through the questions that emerge. When we say that history repeats itself, we really are pointing to the idea that similar questions emerge in different historical moments and it is often those questions that have endured from Greek thought until today. These questions might be as broad as asking how to define the couplet, human rights, to asking specific questions about the fall of great civilizations, what is it that makes a great leader be subsumed by power? Questions related to race relations have re-emerged throughout time. There seems to have always been cases of genocide, slavery, discrimination, and greed and it is historicity that is the announcer of these issues as it acts as a "rhetorical interruption" [21] in the process of what we call history, the things that are no longer in the saying, but the thing that is already said.

Historicity contains prejudices that if we acknowledge their power yet set aside, we invite tradition to live, be enriched, and permit our prejudices to be changed by engaging ongoing interpretation(s). Historicity is open and yet it grounds human consciousness in limits. Questions that emerge from a given historical moment and the responses that occur from those questions permit new possibilities to emerge that perhaps would not have been considered without the revelatory call of the question. We are always altering those limits as we listen for and respond to questions within the particular historical horizon presented by the question because we only understand questions optimally within a particular set of historical circumstances. In this relationship between the communicative agent and the question-response, there is no control of the questions that emerge before us and that call out to us. We have no control of their origin or of their interrogation if us. The full concept of historicity suggests

---

21   Michael J. Hyde, The Call of Conscience: Heidegger and Levinas , Rhetoric, and the Euthanasia Debate (Columbia, SC: University of South Carolina Press, 2001), 77-78.

a temporality that, in its "*futuralness*"[22] is co-present and at the same time, not-yet-been.

Exploration of historicity that acknowledges prejudice is open to interpretive possibilities as a philosophical hermeneutic designed to be accountable and responsible to a given historical moment while privileging the text spoken, written, or observed, situated within particular bias—yet not being persuaded by it. In the next section, the question of this particular historical moment related to transformative leisure is explicitly discussed. Gadamer provides a helpful reminder that ensures adequate and sufficient attention is given to the emergence of questions in any given moment when he suggests, "[a] historical hermeneutics that does not make the *nature of the historical question* the central thing, and does not inquire into a historian's motives in examining historical material, lacks its most important element."[23] In other words, Gadamer reminds us that when engaging historicity the nature of the particular question must be a central focus to the inquiry, lest one diverges toward an inquiry that is based in agency or simply fails to find an appropriate response related to the nature of the question. To ensure this adherence to the nature of the historical question, we should remember that hermeneutical activity opens interpretation and there is always a historically effected consciousness in the *saying* of historicity.

A historically effected consciousness is not just an inquiry into the history of something else. Rather, it includes the trace of something left behind that creates an effect. A historically effected consciousness is a living effect that is not past, though something has occurred, it is alive in the moment of its effect. It is the *saying* of a given historical moment and not the *said*. The idea that the past somehow affects consciousness forces us to apprehend the idea that we are affected by the action of a history that we may or may not have experienced.

Paul Ricoeur does not agree with Gadamer on the idea of a sovereign consciousness and it being a master of meaning. While Ricoeur does not dismiss the notion of a historically effected consciousness, he does dismiss the connection it has to "tradition" in that he argues the term, tradition, has been used to indiscriminately, which has the

---

22 Corey Anton, "Futuralness as Freedom: Moving Toward the Past that Will-Have-Been," in *Media and the Apocalypse*, eds. K. R. Hart and A. M. Holba (New York: Peter Lang, 2009), 189-202.

23 Gadamer, *Truth and Method*, 339.

potential to cause interpretive problems. Ricoeur does offer the notion of a historical consciousness that is situated within a "fusion of horizons" which he suggests more aptly will resolve the linguistic problem of the term tradition.[24] Ricoeur's interpretive concern about the usage of the term *tradition* is helpful, and if we consider tradition as a traditionality, the idea of having temporal distance emerges and separates us from a past that is not dead but rather refers to the idea that we gain meaning from the past.

Understanding the centrality of historicity to a phenomenological inquiry, the first step now is to identify the common sense question(s) of our particular historical moment related to the focus of this book, transformative leisure. Understanding that there is a tradition of literature that begins during the height of Greek civilization that runs through contemporary literature, and in the Introduction a selected and brief discussion of that literature was synthesized, the next step is to identify those questions today that relate to transformative leisure, our quality of life, and our lives a communicative agents.

THE QUESTION OF A GIVEN MOMENT

Most assuredly, the argument of this book is that in contemporary American society, in the nexus of our particular historical moment, there is a continuing atrophy of transformative leisure. This atrophy can be attributed to rapidly changing technologies, keeping up with the upgrades and new versions of these new technologies, and the industry that is more aptly described as a recreation industry but it has linguistically misappropriated the couplet *leisure industry*. Theodor Adorno pointed to this problem in his essay on *Free Time* where he argued that there is no real free time because work and free time do not have a genuine or authentic freedom since one is situated in a social totality in both conditions.[25] Adorno argued that every aspect is socially determined so there is no free time in the sense that imbues transformative leisure experiences. Adorno's concern over the loss of genuine free time exemplifies this notion of the atrophy of leisure.

There are three symptoms of the atrophy of leisure that mark them as a central concern for our time. First, a note about why the descriptor,

24   Paul Ricoeur, *Time and Narrative*, Vol. 3 (Chicago, IL: University of Chicago Press, 1988), 220.

25   Theodor Adorno, "Free Time," *The Culture Industry: Selected Essays on Mass Culture*, ed. J. Bernstein (London: Routledge, 1991).

"atrophy" was selected to ground the identification of a question for this historical moment is necessary. In general, atrophy means a sense of not working properly, a state of laziness perhaps, a lack of something in some way, a degeneration or a decline of a particular something. When we think about it, our muscles become atrophic if they are placed in a cast and we cannot use them. In order to use these muscles again after the cast is removed we often require physical therapy, or a training of sorts that reminds the muscles how to work and it builds up their resistance which prepares them for *normal* usage. In much the same way, the term atrophy related to transformative leisure denotes a degeneration of the engagement of leisure as there has been a decline in the classical understanding of leisure and in the practice of that kind of leisure. On the other hand, there is no real decline in the recreation industry. So, the idea of "atrophy of leisure" seemed most appropriate for this inquiry since it simply means that there is a decline or a degeneration of leisure activities in most American lives today. This rhetorically linguistic shift in the understanding of the term as well as the changing technologies and their rapid upgrades each play a role in the creation of the atrophic condition of transformative leisure today.

Rapid technological changes that have pervaded American culture in the later part of the twentieth century concerned Marshal McLuhan, Neil Postman, Lance Strate and other scholars who, while acknowledging the benefits, also recognized potential problems that could affect how human beings communicate with each other and how they get along in the world together, in general. Thus, this communicative chaos continues to cause new challenges in our world of communicative beings. Media ecologists have this in mind as they study media environments related to human relationships. Neil Postman's book, *Amusing Ourselves to Death: Public Discourse in an Age of Show Business* warns people about becoming addicted to our media environment, especially television, because what is shown on television is only a glimpse at something and that glimpse is not necessary the truth about the thing.[26] Postman did not dismiss television, in fact, he admitted to watching it himself, but his problem with it centered around the notion of thinking what one sees on television as the truth, when it is not the truth. In some ways, he wanted people to be media literate,

---

26   Neil Postman, *Amusing Ourselves to Death: Public Discourse in the Age of Show Business* (New York: Penguin Books, 1985).

to know what it is they are watching and to realize that in general, television is for entertainment, even with new broadcasts, entertainment first, news second.

Keeping up with the rapid technological changes poses challenges that can potentially change the human experience in unforeseen ways. The idea of momentum, eagerness, dispatch, or acceleration is no longer a means to an end for us today. Because of technological advancements, these synonyms have become an end in themselves. Rapid technological changes that our society has become dependent upon, now more than ever should remind us as communicative beings that we need to recall Pieper's message about leisure and reintegrate transformative leisure back into our lives. In the classical sense, transformative leisure is slow and situated within the moment of the experience that is not driven by any concept of chronological time as is in the experience of momentum, eagerness, dispatch, and acceleration. It is with this commitment to the fast-paced, never-ending, and quick actions of technologies and basic daily communicative practices that the eclipse of transformative leisure is revealed and propelled. In order to engage in transformative leisure one must not rush. Any sense of fast-pacedness based upon measurement of chronological time crushes the invitation and opportunity of a truly authentic leisure experience. Because transformative leisure is hard work and because it begins within a quiet contemplative spirit of the actor, it must also accept the implied slowness that accompanies that mindset. It is in the context of slowness that transformative leisure begins.

The value of being slow or the state of slowness can be very uncomfortable for many people, especially since we are in a face paced, movement driven society. A condition of Western societies is increasing marked by sense of unease in both public and private lives. Extending his placement of the sense of unease to the interiority of the human being can more accurately depict what this atrophy of leisure and situatedness within a rapidly changing environment has to say about the effects to the soul, thus creating a need for the recuperation of the soul.

Of course there are different perspectives on the idea of slowness and what it means in a world (at least from a Western experience) of work. For instance, a consequentialist perspective considers the profound consequences that a life outside of slowness has dire consequences to one's health and life satisfaction (or happiness) and a Libertarian perspective focuses on individual self-determination as being essential to the value of slowness.[27] But the real value of slow-ness, or being slow, comes to us from an ontological and phenomeno-logical situatedness in which we experience time and space otherwise. In the play of transformative leisure, slowness cannot be measured because it is not a chronological experience. Rather, slowness is a state of becoming within an experience of play. In other words, if we want to more fully understand the value of what it means to be slow, the idea of slow itself must be revised and removed from a chronological sense of slow versus fast. Therefore, slowness is a state of being or a condition under which transformative leisure is engaged. Movement within a state of slowness doesn't necessarily have to be slow in the sense of a chronological or time-driven slow. The state of slow is a way of being with something else as one contemplates, studies, explores, experiments, and wonders about the-thing-itself or the other.

Finally, the linguistic shift from recreation to leisure in the industry or business of time away from work is the final culprit that contributed to the atrophy of leisure. If we continue to mix up the linguistic sym-bols of recreation and leisure, and since language determines how we think about things, we will not be able to separate the two experiences and find different inherent values of each one. Until public marketing practices and scholarly and trade publications embrace a linguistically focused communicative turn toward the inherent and accurate differ-ences in each linguistic label, Western society will continue along a rhetorical path that reinforces a leisure atrophy in our lives. It is ever more necessary today for a public discussion that reveals these distinc-tions between transformative leisure and recreation, minimizing nei-ther, but rather, illuminating the value of each activity within our lives.

There is a sense of urgency in this linguistic clarification because the world of work and recreation is fast becoming the only two worlds in which we engage ourselves and the other. We have a choice to make the communicative turn toward transformative leisure by exploring leisure from different hermeneutic entrances along with the complexi-ties and nuances that reveal the power and significance transformative leisure brings to our communicative life with ourselves (intraperson-ally) and with others.

---

27   Haney, "The Value of Slow."

CONCLUSION: HERMENEUTIC ENTRANCES (THE WHY)

Humility and commitment go hand in hand, they are partners, and they are counterparts.[28] Interpretive practices require a transversal rationality in which there emerges a play between interlocutors that find ways of communicating despite the challenges of failing to find common ground or fully misinterpreting that which is communicatively exchanged. This implies a hermeneutic humility seeks out commonplaces for open discussion and the engagement of transversal play even in the face of failure to understand misunderstanding and to deliberate contestation between communicative beings.[29]

The idea of a transversal rationality presupposes the replacement of anything universal, which moves beyond the limits of universality and ethnology. In this space of rational transversality one keeps or maintains one's perspective (even if only for a while) while remaining open to the perspective of the by a "humility of transversal comprehension."[30] Positioning one's self within this kind of hermeneutic humility enables communicative beings to effectively and broadly communicate which can act as a gathering agent or a bridge between two sides rather than a divisive tool that ensures the lack of communication, miscommunication, or communication that lacks integrity and honesty. In other words, one meets the other in this space of rational transversality through hermeneutic humility.

Hermeneutic humility is not always easy to achieve—in fact, it finds us if we let it. It is essential for the communicative being to understand hermeneutic humility because human beings must live with and among other human beings. Living life with transformative leisure as a practice enables communicative beings existence within the space of transversal rationality, a portal to open our world of thought and action. Transversal rationality is a dynamic experience of the senses that exhibit a "lying across, extending over, intersecting, meeting and

---

28   Calvin O. Schrag, R. E. Ramsey, "Method and Phenomenological Research: Humility and Commitment in Interpretation," *Human Studies* 17 (1994): 131-137.

29   Schrag and Ramsey, "Method and Phenomenological Research."

30   Schrag and Ramsey, "Method and Phenomenological Research," 135.

converging without achieving coincidence." [31] In other words, this implies an interrelated experience of to and fro between various perspectives and actions that opens our minds through play and replay; the building and rebuilding of ideas. In transformative leisure, one engages this kind of open humility necessary for authentic and successful communicative action. This mode of communication has unforeseen outcomes that lead us toward the elevation of our soul, thus removing us from the toxicity of fast-paced and technologically fabricated world. Contemplative actions *do* more than outwardly, physical actions for our soul or interiority. Contemplation elevates our soul and is responsible for raising our ability to experience inner cultivation.

The action of contemplation has significant implications to the human communicative spirit yet similar to Martin Buber's genuine dialogue and the dialogic moment of "the between"[32] communicative beings cannot permanently be in these kinds of states. Contemplative actions are necessary and fundamental to learning and experiencing hermeneutic humility and ultimately prepare us for transversal rationality within a communicative space. Hermeneutic humility permits things to show themselves to us—we see these things in their showing and this permits us to respond appropriately.

It is within this spirit of hermeneutic humility that we look toward finding other perspectives from which we can learn about and engage transformative leisure. We know now what has happened in society to some extent that has caused a question to emerge that points us toward a revisioning of how leisure is understood and engaged by individuals and collective communities. We understand through this humility that we must open our senses to the experience and implications of leisure to our life world. So that we do not compartmentalize our understanding of transformative leisure, we look for different ways of thinking about it through the actual engagement, experience, and the implications that follow both contemplative and publically experienced communicative actions of leisure.

Whether transformative leisure is explored from a phenomenological perspective or an existential perspective (to name just two) and

---

31 Calvin O. Schrag, *The Resources of Rationality: A Response to the Postmodern Challenge* (Bloomington, IN: Indiana University Press, 1992), 149.

32 Martin Buber, *Between Man and Man* (New York: Macmillan Publishing, 1965).

while these perspectives might even be contradictory at times, our hermeneutic comprehension grows and is shaped by these multiple perspectives in ways that open comprehensive potentiality. We learn from each new perspective and with each unique reflection on transformative leisure we increase our abilities to engage transversal rationality. By opening ourselves to different hermeneutic entrances as we consider transformative leisure, we enter the ongoing conversation and in doing so, transformative leisure can be a way toward a philosophical life in a world of unrelenting work in both public and private realms; together we can reshape how we think about leisure as a way of life. The next chapter invites us to do just that, reshape how we think about leisure through a phenomenological lens that offers a perspective from a variety of vantage points.

CHAPTER 2

TRANSFORMATIVE LEISURE IN ACTION

We want to make consciousness equal with the whole of experience, to gather into consciousness for-itself (pour soi) all the life of consciousness in-itself (en soi).

—Maurice Merleau-Ponty

There is no phenomenological result apart from the experience through which it comes about, in which it remains essentially open to its own history and intersubjectivity of interpretation and critique.

—John O'Neill

To talk about transformative leisure in action I must consider action as part of the experience. Remember that in chapter 1, *Transformative Leisure in Discourse*, I considered that transformative leisure in discourse pointed toward narratives in which it is experienced. The notion of narratival discourse sets the stage for this chapter in that transformative leisure moves from a leisure in discourse to a leisure in lived action. This chapter explores the experience of transformative leisure and the experience of the self situated within narratival conditions of action. Narratives are ontological structures that are shaped by the self, the self in relation to other selves, and the conditions of the environment in which selves are embedded and entrusted together. Action itself is enacted by a subject who has her or his own perception of the particular action(s) and its place or significance to the story in which she or he is embedded. Action can be described as phenomena occurring in relation to our attention and disclosedness. The action in transformative leisure is a phenomenological event that enables us a particular understanding. Consequently, a brief consideration of how I think about phenomenology opens this chapter so that transformative leisure can be explored phenomenologically. Because this chapter focuses on action, I end the chapter moving into transformative leisure as an ontological becoming of a virtue ethic in action.

Phenomenology is a kind of methodological inquiry that studies human experience by asking questions about what and how things present themselves to us. Phenomenology is also a philosophical movement of sorts that invites one to think philosophically in perhaps a different way than other kinds of philosophical approaches. There are several excellent historical overviews that are more like historical surveys of this movement that can offer a textured understanding but for now, we can begin with Edmund Husserl (1859-1938) who provides us with a starting place to talk about phenomenology. Many contemporary phenomenologists begin with his *Logical Investigations* because it was the initial statement revealing this philosophical mode of examination. Since Husserl's *Investigations*, philosophers have further developed his early ideas into a field of rich and textured ways of thinking about and attempts at understanding human experience. However, we know that understanding is always incomplete, which is what makes phenomenology so interesting and yet, so challenging. This is also a reason to remember humility and commitment in one's methodological approach because these qualities permit "holistic understanding and analytical explanation." [1] A phenomenological perspective might feel like one is only looking at a part but instead, it permits us to see what we could-not-before or have-not-yet. First, I consider aspects of phenomenological inquiry and second, I consider transformative leisure through a phenomenological lens.

Appearances alone continue to make phenomenology relevant especially today in our image driven world and virtual spaces of human existence. Mass technologies have fragmented these appearances even more so than before they invaded our everyday existence. Appearances come and go; appear and disappear; and change and shift our perception of things. Appearances create a technological fragmentation of parts and wholes, identity in manifold, and presence and absence in interplay together. Aside from appearances, intentionality is another central aspect of this method of inquiry because it has to do

1   Schrag and Ramsey, "Method and Phenomenological Research," 132.

with consciousness of, or an experience with, something. It is what our attention is directed toward, whether it is an object we see or an object we imagine, or an object we remember. Therefore, every act of intending has its intending object. This sense of "intend" or "intention" is not the same, as the "intention" that we have in mind when we act.[2] Rather, in this case, intend or intention is concerned with one's focus of attention or intention, to have a conscious relationship to an object or to-the-thing-itself.

Part of phenomenological inquiry includes the idea of reduction in which the philosopher turns away from the thing toward the meaning of the thing. This is a matter of turning from the scientific objectified meaning to a meaning that is immediate and experienced in a life-world. There are six commonalities that can be universally applied to the phenomenological method: 1) since most phenomenologists agree that there is a difference between the natural world and the philosophical attitude, so there is a difference between philosophy and science. This then accounts for two perspectives found within this phenomenological movement that phenomenology is concerned with questions of epistemology and the position that phenomenology is concerned with questions of ontology; 2) Even with this first difference mentioned above, there is a necessary and complex relationship between science and philosophy; 3) reduction is a necessary part of phenomenology but each phenomenologist will engage reduction differently, some radically and others lightly; 4) intentionality is central to a phenomenological approach in philosophy; 5) phenomenology is focused on exploring the question about meaning and Being of beings and how Being of beings and the Being of the world are constituted; finally, a level of "intuitionism" is essential and part of phenomenological inquiry that manifests in a primordial form, this is what Husserl refers to as the principle of all principles.[3] Acknowledging these characteristics of a general phenomenology, it becomes clear that the potential of

---

2   Perhaps such as when there is legal argument about the intentions of someone charged with murder or manslaughter. In this case, intentionality is used to make a distinction under the law that would have influence upon sentencing and other conditions related to the criminal justice system. This is a category for argumentation and sometimes the "intention" that is argued in court is not the actual intention that is experienced.

3   Robert Audi, ed. *The Cambridge Dictionary of Philosophy* (New York: Cambridge University Press, 1999).

multiple phenomenologies exists. This potential becomes more obvious when transformative leisure is discussed later through the lens of phenomenology and our perceptions.

Phenomenology leads us to the question of perception. Traditional analyses of perception, that which began with the notion of sensation, is incorrect or incomplete.[4] I consider the phenomenological experience of the *making* or *doing* of transformative leisure specifically through the interplay and co-existence of presence and absence. Without this interplay the *doing* of transformative leisure is left incomplete and can potentially lead to the creation of a false consciousness. Presence and absence both must be negotiated in our perceptions as counterparts.

Perception

There are multiple theories of perception that consider one or more of the following three principles, the common factor principle, the phenomenal principle, and the representational principle. Most theories negotiate one or more of these principles for a variety of reasons. Generally, the common factor principle begins from the assumption that different experiences are more or less correct or successful. This principle appeals to everyday visual experiences. The phenomenal principle asserts, within an if-then format, that if there is something that sensibly appears before me (such as a red violin) then there is something that exists which I am aware posses the quality of a red violin. Finally, the representational principle argues that all visual experiences are either intentional (in that your attention is drawn to something deliberately) or representational.[5] Despite the plausibility of these principles, they are found to be incomplete or inadequate to fully account for perception for reasons that include epistemological or metaphysical contradictions to sense data we perceive.

Perception is the origin of the world. The idea of the primacy of perception means "that the experience of perception is our presence at the moment when things, truths, [and] values are constituted."[6] Perception teaches us objectivity and it calls us toward tasks of knowledge and action. Perception is a privileged realm of experience because

---

4   Maurice Merleau-Ponty, *Phenomenology of Perception* (London: Routledge & Kegan Paul, 1967; 1962).

5   William Fish, *Philosophy of Perception: A Contemporary Introduction* (New York: Routledge, 2010).

6   Maurice Merleau-Ponty, *Primacy of Perception* (Evanston, IL: Northwestern University Press, 1975; 1964), 25.

it is primordial yet that does not mean everything else is derived from perception though it does reveal that our perceptions re-create and contribute to the making of our world through our engagement with interrelationships between people and objects in the practical human realm. Therefore, the world is not a place where human experience occurs, rather, the world is the place in which one turns toward in experience.[7] Perception is not limited to a response to exterior stimuli rather, in perception we implicate ourselves into perceptual behaviors so that we can analyze the relationship between ourselves, our bodies, and the world. Another way to understand the relationship between the subject, its body, and its world is to consider this relationship in space. Merleau-Ponty stated:

> Our body is not in space like things; it inhabits or haunts space. It applies itself to space like a hand to an instrument, and when we wish to move about we do not move the body as we move an object. We transport it without instruments as if by magic, since it is ours and because through it we have direct access to space. For us the body is much more than an instrument or a means; it is our expression in the world, the visible form of our intentions.[8]

From this description of the spatial relationships in perception, it becomes clear that we engage perception in the life-world or the lived world as a conscious activity in which the object is constituted. Perception is not something that once happened but it is living experience that constitutes being in its action. Perception is experienced within a particular horizon and this experience is "in action" which means it is an engagement within texture instead of a once-knowing occurrence or a flat engagement outside of a context. Perception is the original modality of consciousness. Consciousness does not really begin to exist until it sets limits on to an object—it is not private. In private, consciousness has nothing to which to attend and is therefore, chaos, which is nothingness. Perception reveals an interrelationship between a person and a thing which points to *how* perception occurs and what perception does.

---

7   D. Carr, "Maurice Merleau-Ponty: Incarnate Consciousness," in *Existential Philosophers: Kierkegaard to Merleau-Ponty* ed. G. A. Schrader (New York: MacGraw-Hill, 1967), 369-430.

8   Merleau-Ponty, *Primacy*, 5.

Sensations, then, are not the object we sense but they are instead in the experience between ourselves and the object. The perceptual something is always in the middle of something else and is constituted and embedded within a particular field. In evaluating perception it is the quality of sense-data that shapes a particular part of our experience. Therefore, there is no clear thing as pure sensation because it is actually the property of a particular object and a happening in the middle of a field between ourselves and an object that defines what a sensation means. To better understand how perception is informed by experience and how it shapes experience, a consideration of the interplay of presence and absence assists this discovery.

PRESENCE AND ABSENCE

The idea of being present does not simply mean being somewhere with something else at the same time but it means more so to be present in participation with something else. Presence means a participation that is immediately in life. To understand something does not necessarily mean to reason or come to judgment after setting forth a logically well-reasoned assertion. Rather it means to have a present involvement in the idea or thing that is being said. This is not a relationship between persons or between a reader and an author but it is a sharing in what the text (written or spoken) shares with us. To explore presence and absence related to transformative leisure, the aspects of anticipation, cointending, attention, and appearance help us. We experience a perception within a particular horizon that is already in action in which we are already presently and immediately involved. Our perceptions inescapably include, involve, and negotiate presences and absences in a lived moment or moments. We engage them through the action of cointending.

COINTENDING

When Merleau-Ponty clarified his perspective on presence in perception he provided an example in which he states:

> [i]f we consider an object which we perceive but one of whose sides we do not see, or if we consider objects which are not within our visual field at the moment—i.e., what is happening behind our back or what is happening in America or at the South Pole— how

should we describe the existence of these absent objects or the non-visible parts of present objects?[9]

In this example Merleau-Ponty pointed out that we cannot consider these as representations because we cannot see these things before us so we do not actually perceive it. What we have is a possibility of something. However, if we look at a lamp, we perceive it but we cannot see the whole thing, rather, one part of it is hidden from our perception. When we anticipate the unseen part of what we see, in this case, the lamp, we cointend its existence. While we can anticipate the unseen of the perceived object, we still do not have proof of the object's truth. We merely have a perception of the presence of something. So, when talking about perception we must be careful to not make assumptions about them otherwise we become diverted from the *truth* or we create a mistruth. When we negotiate presence and absence as an interplay we perhaps do not have truths such as in mathematical proofs but we do have are presences that point toward a truth, but not Truth itself.

These experiences with perception indicate a new modality in perception, in that it is neither the ideal being nor a simplistic sensory event of experience. Rather, the modality involves a sense of gestalt. In gestalt theory it would be difficult to break down a perception into sensory parts because the whole is prior to the parts and the whole is not an ideal whole. If we were to break down this perception we would not recognize the whole, in this case, the whole has more meaning and is more valuable than the sum of the parts. It is the synthesis of the perception that constitutes its unity that gives meaning. Perceptions are thus, paradoxical. The thing that is perceived only exists then, when one perceives it. If we imagine a place that has never been seen, the fact that we imagine it makes us present in the place. Consider the musical *Brigadoon*. The place of Brigadoon does not exist until it is perceived by a human being. At the moment of perception the mythical/mystical village comes into existence. At the moment of perceiving the existence of this village, the perceiver is in the presence of it. This constitutes a paradox of immanence and transcendence in perception; immanence because the perceived object is not alien to the one who perceives and transcendence because the perceived object is always comprised of something more than what is present. So, when we produce this perceptual experience in our thought, we are required

---

9   Ibid., 13.

to have both presence and absence in the experience, which are not contradictory aspects, but complementary aspects of experience.

Presence and absence are original and formal structures in phenomenology that are ontologically interwoven.[10] Presences are not just presences but they are present to tell us something that can help to restore meaning that we lose from our own internal world or from our philosophical confusion. When we perceive a material object we see the object from one angle and one perspective. We cannot see all sides of the object at once. For example, when I see my violin I see only part of it. I cannot see the back or the sides of my instrument. I cannot see the inner or inside dimensions of my violin, in fact, I cannot see the sound post inside the instrument yet this sound post is responsible for the kind of sound that emerges from the violin. In order to *fully perceive* the object we need to see all sides of the object at once. What we do then, is to perceive by cointending the sides that we cannot humanly see. This is a cointending of presence and absence of the object. Our perception is a blending of what we see and what we intend – or do not see. We are at present with the whole violin but we embrace the absence of the sides, back, and inside that we cannot see – this is a cointention of absence.

Absence includes things that are absent because they are of the future, they have not happened yet, they are in a state of futuralness, or forgotten, or concealed, or secret, or beyond our comprehension. In thinking about presence and absence we might think that presences are more important than absences or things we cannot see but that is simply not true. While we think that presences are more familiar to us than absences we never fully realize a presence without an absence and vice versa. They coexist and give life to each other.

Let me give an example of this. When someone dies in your life you experience an absence, you no longer physically *see* that person, perhaps you even conceal this loss from others, perhaps you begin to forget about the person, you forget the sound of his/her laughter or you begin to forget the lines of his/her face. This is an absence in the sense that you no longer comprehend these things yet there are moments of remembrance from a sight, sound, scent, or observation. Then that person is everpresent with you, an image in your mind, a thought, a memory of an experience. You are engaging the presence with that

10   Robert Sokolowski, *Introduction to Phenomenology* (NY: Cambridge University Press, 2000).

image, thought, or observation that bring this presence into our perceptual field. You are cointending what is not there yet everpresent in your experience at that given moment. This is a play of presence and absence and you experience this through a cointending of the-thing-it-self—that person.

Critics of the cointending of presence and absence perspective argue that there is a conflict in reasoning, which is that a co-constitution of presence and absence when the *here and now* drive absence into the *there and then* – should serve to keep them a part. This interplay of presence and absence has been criticized as being problematic because absence means "absence, otherness, and motion" fail to gain respective importance, therefore absence cannot co-constitute presence.[11] But this argument cannot stand because you cannot begin with the assumption that absence presupposes a lower importance. Perhaps they fall into what Martin Buber would refer to as the unity of contraries.[12] Nevertheless, without the absence there would be no presence, and consequently, a lack of human ability to perceive.

In contemplation there is a pure presence that provides a key for understanding some less complete knowledge and experience that is absent. Presence in this regard is organic and natural to human nature. Martin Heidegger's notion of Being drives thinking and contemplation and consequently we are *becoming* through this action.[13] We are in a mindful presence and at the same time attending to an absence. The interplay between presence and absence permits us to analyze our thinking and truthfulness. In this interplay of presence and absence we then name things and that action enables us to bring ourselves and others to truth(s).

In case my argument for the interplay of presence and absence does not yet cohere as a possibility, it would be interesting to consider the idea that impressions have a derivative presence, much like Emmanuel Levinas's "derivative I" which means the "I" comes into being through the Other, so images could have a derivative presence meaning they come into being by the presence of their absence and the presencing

11   E. S. Casey, "On the Issue of Presence," *Journal of Philosophy* 77, no. 10 (1980): 644.

12   Martin Buber, *The Knowledge of Man: A Philosophy of the Interhuman* (New York: Harper and Row, 1966).

13   Heidegger considers thinking and contemplation as a mindfulness or an attentiveness.

in perception that which gives the impressions a type of existence.[14] It could be interpreted that these images have a deviated presence rather than an original presence. A deviated presence is a presence that emerged or deviated from something else, perhaps organically, in so far that intentionality is questionable. So whether one finds the presence of an image to be derivative or deviated, there is still some constructive kinship regarding images in general that the idea of the interplay of presence and absence creates a synthesis of empty and filled intentions. The present is isolated from the past.[15] Present domination is a concept that describes the operative principle that guides actions, it means that one is driven by a pulse of the immediate. Present domination occurs when we are in the moment where we cointend and as we cointend, our attention is engaged.

ATTENTION

Attention in consciousness is awakened and developed by our perception. In our attention, we perceive what is already there, the attention does not create it. Attention actually creates nothing though it acts like a search light in total darkness and it is deduced from the priority of the objective world in which it is engaged. In short, we perceive objects or sensations that are already there and by doing so, the thing-itself is revealed from within darkness, and this revelation is *attention*. A secondary attention, which is a recalling of knowledge that we had already gained or had already been revealed to us in a previous attention becomes important as we consider presence and absence because, "to pay attention is not merely further to elucidate pre-existing data, it is to bring about a new articulation of them by taking them as figures."[16] In other words, attention and secondary attention are preformed as horizons that come into our intellectual consciousness. Attention is not a recollection of pictorial representations but it is an active development of something new which makes a clear and explicit implication of itself moving from the indeterminate horizon into an active perceptual range. Attention reveals an immediacy that gives life to the

14   Ronald C. Arnett, "The Responsive 'I': Levinas's Derivative Argument," *Argumentation & Advocacy* 40, no. 1 (2003): 39.

15   Edmund Husserl, *The Crisis of European Sciences and Transcendental Phenomenology: An Introduction to Phenomenological Philosophy* (Evanston, IL: Northwestern University, 1970).

16   Merleau-Ponty, *Phenomenology of Perception*, 30.

experience itself. This is a reflection in play where consciousness meets the face of its own unreflective life in order to be awakened to something. In other words, attention is alive and gives life to something that is existent and fixed in a totality that ultimately takes life.

In consideration of consciousness, the question that emerges involves asking about the relationship between intellectual consciousness and perceptual consciousness. The notion of a true perception is consistent with a truth in intellectual consciousness since our experience and our knowledge have the same structures and the same kind of horizons in our perceptual experience. This truth in perception and truth in intellectual knowledge is an approximate truth since it cannot be isolated from external encounters. The aspect of attention is met within intellectual consciousness that is an approximate attention. The idea of attending to-the-thing-itself is albeit awkward or an inconsistent idea if we think about it. This would mean that when our attention moves toward something, it moves in an intellectual openness that is met within dialogic circumstances, with itself and with others. So, our attention is confronted and diverted to something else, to some other essence. Our attention is met with otherness, intellectual consciousness, and so it is interrupted from the-thing-itself.

In the intellectual consciousness, presence and absence interplay in pure reflexion, situated outside of perception. At this point we are no longer a perceiving subject; we have become a thinking subject. This initially sounds like an agreement of sorts with Descartes' mind body split, however, it is not. In Merleau-Ponty's notion of the "I," or *cogito*, the act of doubting in reflexion understands itself as a doubting entity which means it cannot doubt itself if it recognizes itself doubts. The very fact of doubting eliminates the possibility of doubt. This is an important distinction about reflexion and attention in perception which goes back to the interplay between presence and absence, in that in our perception we must be absent to ourselves in order to doubt. In this absence, presence emerges as the doubting obstructs its own negation. Our intellectual consciousness is in reflexion of the interplay of absence and presence which is the aspect of attention in perception. To texture the notion of attention related to presence and absence a look at other perspectives is helpful. These differing notions can help us to further see connections between attention and presence and absence.

Presence and absence have been considered through the metaphor of attention.[17] Simone Weil suggested that we need self-diminishment (which is absence) to have a higher level of attention or attentive presence. Weil described these higher forms of attention as a synthesis of divine absence and divine presence. So, we cannot have presence without absence. Weil's angst emerged when she realized a fulfillment of attention toward something involves the notion of a nothingness of the personal self.

Attention has four forms: 1) intellectual, that is, intellectual exercises and apprehension of truth; 2) supernatural attention, which refers to intending God's presence in the world; 3) love of neighbor which involves human freedom and realization of personhood; and 4) affliction which represents brutality of overcoming of the ego by violence in an indifferent world.[18] As Weil discovered these forms of attention she revealed that the apprehension of absence brings these forms closer to perfection. Weil provided an example of the image of Christ as it points to absence while in overabundance of presence of love – the love that consents to suffer. This notion of attention also resonates with Holy week during the Easter season in the Catholic faith. During holy week, as the death and resurrection of Christ is remembered, the crucifixes and icons of Joseph and Mary that frame the altar area of the church are covered in purple cloth. One's attention is drawn to the absence of Christ while at the same time Christians anticipate the celebration of his presence or resurrection (figurative and literal). It is known or anticipated that on Easter day the purple cloth will be removed and the presence of Christ will be revealed again. The presence was always-already in existence yet the absence pervaded that existence for a while. It is the experience of that purple cloth that points our attention to the presence and absence of Christ and perhaps a larger spiritual experience. The presence of Christ is pointed to as attention is given to the cloth and His image is "heard full of silence."[19] To make this clearer, attention is something more akin to a revelation, an unveiling, a calling, or a disclosedness.

Heidegger's use of the term attention relates more to an awareness of something else or a kind of consciousness. For example, in Heidegger's

---

17   Simone Weil, *Gravity and Grace* (London: Routledge, 1952).

18   Simone Weil, *Waiting for God* (New York: Harper and Row, 1973).

19   A. Pirruccello, "Interpreting Simone Weil: Presence and Absence in Attention," *Philosophy East and West* 45, no. 1 (1995): 75.

consideration of *Dasein*, he stated "it must unveil a primordial kind of Being of *Dasein* in such a way, indeed, that from this kind of Being the phenomenon of thrownness, to which we have called attention, can be exhibited in its existential concreteness." [20] Attention for Heidegger points us toward something, a disclosedness of something. In each of these considerations of attention in presence and absence, our perception becomes a central aspect because we become within the experience. Attention, whether a disclosedness (Heidegger); a present reality of absence (Weil); or an intellectual consciousness (Merleau-Ponty), is a necessary aspect of presence and absence that infiltrates our perception and our perceptioning. Attention does not create the perception but it does direct us toward a place to perceive. Attention permits us to experience a consciousness perception and reflexion toward an intellectual consciousness which is necessary for the engagement of transformative leisure. To continue this exploration, an examination of appearances shapes our understanding and experience further.

APPEARANCE

Appearance is a phenomenon of consciousness and it is structurally different than illusion. Appearances possess a sensory characteristic that is incontestable and are not required to exist within a horizon of meaning. In fact, according to Merleau-Ponty, appearances can be an imitation, an interval between something else, an illumination of consciousness, or something other than reality. Appearances can be true appearances or false appearances or they can be appearances that are of a different reality and therefore, neither true or false. A false appearance has potential to hide present reality just as likely as the true appearance has the potential to unveil or reveal the true present reality. Appearances are situated in sense experience and can be distinguished from judgment in that there is no commitment assigned to an appearance, unlike in judgment one takes a measured stand. Appearances should be taken at face value and they should not try to be possessed or owned.

Merleau-Ponty described this aspect of appearance in his example of a cardboard box:

---

20   Martin Heidegger, *Being and Time* (San Francisco, CA: Harper Collins, 1962).

A large cardboard box seems heavier to me than a small one made of the same cardboard, and if I confine myself to phenomena I should say that I can in advance *feel* it heavier in my hand. But intellectualism delimits sense experience by the action of a real stimulus on my body. Since here there is none, we have to say that the box is not felt but judged to be heavier, and this example which seemed ready-made to show the sensory aspect of illusion serves on the contrary to prove that there is no sensory knowledge, and that we feel as we judge.[21]

In this case the cardboard box is not measured but we take at face value the size of the box and consider the appearance as sense experience that we draw a conclusion about. In the phenomenal field of perception, appearance happens before a judgment. Appearances can be temporary, involuntary, in between objects, and outside of a horizon. Language and experience provide a truth that is offered through their appearance that is temporal and brings the abstract into a knowing.

Constancy in perception is important in the analysis of appearances. So, it would be important to consider appearances against or in relation to constants because even though appearances come and go into our perceptual range, they are dependent upon constant properties of existence. We come to know these constants through interference of appearances and the inadequacy of appearances; the constants never constitute the appearance in totality. Appearances themselves interplay among constants and are temporal in nature adding to the problem and the primacy of perception. Heidegger offers helpful insight to texture our understanding and point the way toward linking absence and presence to the action of transformative leisure.

Appearance has a double meaning in that "appearing, in the sense of announcing itself, as not-showing-itself; and next, that which does the announcing . . . that which in its showing-itself indicates something which does not show itself."[22] So, appearances reveal a referential relation in beings themselves when it can only be fulfilling when it shows itself. Heidegger tells us that when considering temporality, the "past" means that something is no longer present or that while something is certainly present, it has no effect on the present. However, while this might be true, the past has extraordinary ambiguity in that it belonged to an earlier time that can also belong to the present time, for exam-

21   Merleau-Ponty, *Phenomenology of Perception*, 34.
22   Heidegger, *Being*, 53.

ple, the remains of a Greek temple. In this case, the present cannot be understood without acknowledging the past or what is absent.

Historically, appearances have challenged us as some of the Sophists used and manipulated appearances through the persuasiveness of words to teach and persuade people about something. Appearances are generated through words that are spoken or written, or imaged, delivered through microphones or other electronic channels. In a post-modern era where different modes of communication pervade society, our fascination with appearances becomes at once intense and at once negated. By being confronted with appearances in all of this massness, we begin to become just as fragmented as the appearance stimuli itself. Our attention spans plummet and our interest becomes disengaged. As a result, messages, experiences, and relationships have the potential to fall into only appearances and remain fragmented expelled by a sea of fragmentation, fragments without wholes, multiple absences without an enduring presence. Yet, in phenomenology, we insist that parts can only be understood against the backdrop of the appropriate wholes and that absences make no sense without the presences. So we must search for this exchange in appearances against their whole and we look for connections that help to fill-in our understandings. So not only do we think of the things that are given to us in our experiences but we must also understand ourselves as thinking about those things. In other words, we must look at the appearances against the larger story and be aware we are thinking about them—we are fully present.

Through the metaphors of cointending, attention, and appearance we see that there is a relationship between, among and around presence and absence. By our lack of seeing we actually see; we cannot see without the interplay between presence and absence of sight. Presence burdens our time and space. Absence is adaptable and versatile because there are many types that open a philosophical space where presence is contingent. Presence and absence are independent and yet co-existents. Looking at presence and absence through cointending, attention, and appearance, we can begin to understand the action in transformative leisure where they coexist in the contemplative play that foregrounds the internal/external action or doing and they are at the same time interdependent aspects in the emerging play.

PRESENCE AND ABSENCE IN
TRANSFORMATIVE LEISURE

As discussed previously, transformative leisure goes beyond the daily negotiation of everydayness. Transformative leisure involves an attitude of contemplative celebration that affirms basic meaningfulness of life. Transformative leisure is hard work that begins intellectually in a contemplative fashion. It is driven by an aesthetic sensibility that does not succumb to competition or seek out a particular end. Rather, it is an activity that is conducted for the sake of the activity itself. Transformative leisure is both private and public; it is both experience and potential. Transformative leisure acknowledges the absence of the physical and the presence of the metaphysical. One begins transformative leisure in private, within the interior of one's thoughts. One then experiences transformative leisure in all of its embodied complexities resulting in a serendipitous outcome in some public way. The outcome is unexpected and unplanned. There is a phenomenological ontological involvement that keeps transformative leisure in the abstract yet one knows when one does it or when it is in one's presence and one ought to know when one doesn't do it, when it is absent.

If we recall from chapter one, recreation can be considered a coffee break—or a short term break from daily work. In recreation, one never leaves the world; the world is always present. In transformative leisure, absence and presence must co-exist because when one is engaging leisure one is absent from the present world and attending to-the-thing-itself in a way that obscures the world at the same time, yet one is fully present in the engagement with the-thing-itself. This provides long-term cultivation, something that recreation can never do because in recreation one is everpresent in the world, situated within the absence of philosophical attention, and driven by a concern toward measured outcomes.

For example: I play the violin. I cointend much of my instrument. I cannot see my sound post as it rests beneath one of my f-holes and it touches the inside of the top and bottom of my instrument. It is an absence that I experience, I am aware of it, I feel it, I know it because it makes itself known to me through the sound that emerges when I pull the bow across the strings which permits the sound post to vibrate and make sound. When I play my violin I cannot see my peg box that holds my pegs and maintains the pressure on my strings so that when

I move my bow across them and make a sound, the strings remain tight and in tune which permits me to remain on pitch. I cointend this space because it is an absence that I am aware of. It makes itself known to me for if it was not there I could not play as my strings would not hold tension and my bow could not induce the necessary vibrations for sound to emerge. I cannot see it and it is absent to me so I must cointend it.

To play my instrument I must have attention toward several things. My focus of attention is paramount to whether or not sound comes out of my instrument in a *poiesis* of the aesthetic. I tend to my bow, I hold my bow in my right hand and I bend my right thumb and place it in the intersection of the frog and the stick. I place my right hand fingers in their natural place on the top of my bow stick, making sure to bend my little finger. Without that bending I will not be able to balance my bow, the sound will be harsh and I will not have the right amount of pressure on my bow to pull across the string and make sound with my violin. But I also must give attention to where I put my bow on the string; to close to the bridge and it sounds scratchy, too far from the bridge and my sound becomes tentative, mousy, and almost atonal. I attend to all of these and more phenomena through presence and absence. I do not "see" my bow as I play. I cannot see my bow hand but I must attend to my finger placements. I tend to this through a present attention of the absence and I feel my experience in darkness of absence yet knowing it is everpresent in my temporality. I also cannot be totally present when I put my bow on the string and hope it is not to close or too far from the bridge. I experience this attention through the everpresent absence of its presentness; I not only cointend these things, I must give them an intellectual attention simultaneously as I am in the experience and in the temporal relation these aspects must coexist. Together they will bring meaning and more experience, always changing and always testing me, my attention and my cointending.

Finally, appearances in my violin playing compete for my attention and my cointending. Appearances of musical syntax, markings, bowings, and accidentals in the music interplays with my instrumental voice as it fits within a quartet or a larger symphonic entity. Appearances involve stimuli competing for my attention always emerging as I negotiate my instrument, as I read music, as I play from memory, as I improvise, as I play scales and modulate through keys. Appearances challenge me as they are coming into my experience as fragments but I attend and cointend to them and put them together. I do this and I think about the things I am at play with but I also understand that I am at the same time thinking about myself attending to these experiences. I am in the embodied awareness of both absence and presence in my play. Absence and presence permit me to get lost in my experience as I attend to these phenomena; the material world is not part of that experience. I do not get paid for doing this, I am not "required" to do this, I have no connection to any material thing as I engage transformative leisure; I am lost in the play of presence and absence of appearances.

Phenomenologically, transformative leisure is concerned with the "here and now" of a presence that acknowledges a thing is at once present and absent. Yehudi Menuhin (1916-1999), one of the greatest violinists from the twentieth century, once commented that once you play a note it is gone, absent from existence yet everpresent in your experience. There is a permanence of change in music that is always ontologically present and absent because the note ceases to exist yet it remains presently absent and often leads to the next note (especially in scales but typically in modulations and development sections of musical compositions such as sonata ABA forms). As we experience this "here and now" we are concerned with our relationship to the "here and now" as our place within that experience. Phenomenologically, transformative leisure is not concerned with objects pointed to but the object as it is pointed out; it is the interiority of the external experience that becomes paramount. In playing a scale or a musical phrase, each note as it is perceived points toward the next note. In transformative leisure, the phenomenal moment occurs as I play the note pointing to the next. It is in the pointing that a phenomenological experience occurs. The pointing as-ness creates a phenomenally dynamic perceptive dimension.

The phenomenological experience of transformative leisure involves cointending, attention, appearances, resulting in the aspect of as-ness. Transformative leisure is folded within kairotic moments that lend to the potentiality in timeliness of the thought or action and the transformative aspect of the past, present, and future experiences. These experiences are not limited to traditional aesthetic sensibilities like music, art, writing, or acting. Experiences of transformative leisure can be any kind of activity ranging from fishing, carpentry, rebuilding a car engine, baking whoopee pies, riding a motorcycle, wood carving, reading, or just about any other activity that one approaches in the spirit of contemplation without expected or intended outcomes.

The key to the difference between transformative leisure and work or transformative leisure and recreation involves the contemplative spirit and the outcome. In work, we are often governed by *chronos* and are held to particular and predetermined outcomes. Whether we work on projects in a corporate setting or work in state government, we are governed by time constraints, social and political limitations, and resources imposed upon us by others. As Karl Marx might agree as indicated in a later chapter, when we work for other people, they own our labor and they own us; our time is not our own. While we may be compensated generally for our work, we are also alienated from our work and its' potential. Even if we are self-employed, we still must work within time constraints and with a predetermined expected outcome. In these cases, engaging the work for the sake of itself is generally not possible.

In experiences of transformative leisure, the contemplative starting place allows for the play between presence and absence through cointending the experience, being responsive in our attention, and acknowledging appearances as they come and go, appear and disappear, and move around as ideas develop. These aspects bring together the experience of *as-ness* so that one is open to potentiality that permits an unconstrained seeing. The ability to see *as-ness* in environments that rest outside of transformative leisure is obscured by the focused and intended outcomes as they exist and confront the acting person. *As-ness* does not occur similarly in recreation. In recreation the notes are pointed to in order to get something else; it is a linear experience that focuses on the *getting there* instead of the *as-ness*.

Playing the violin for recreation is a healthy and fun activity but it is very different from playing the violin as transformative leisure. The notion of cointending in recreation does not exist as it does in transformative leisure. For example, in transformative leisure as I stated earlier, I cointend my sound post and my peg box. In recreation the sound post and peg box are not tended to in this sense. In recreation, the sound post and peg box are more likely to be taken for granted and the player might never think about or learn about the architectonics of the instrument and the experience of making sounds. One's focus is not on these aspects because one is more interested in something else such as the social outcome of playing, earning a fee, or trying to impress other people.

Likewise, in recreation, attention is not understood in the same way as it is in transformative leisure. In playing the violin as recreation, my attention might appear as one thing but really be something else. As I sit there in orchestra or as I stand and play in my private home, my posture might indicate I am paying attention to the music but I am more likely to be thinking about what I need to do next, when rehearsal is over, or why can't I sit in the first stand (and make judgments about other people and how they play instead of evaluating my own playing seriously). Some of this attention is governed by jealousy and coveting what other people have and some might be governed by a more carefree or careless attitude. Regardless of the *why* that situates our attentiveness or lack of attentiveness, we can still have fun playing the violin for recreation. The key to attention is that one must be inside a phenomenological location—to be inside the music and physical action of playing the instrument in an embodied movement of play. In recreation, one is never inside because the elements of cointending, attention, and now appearance are not experienced in the same way or at all.

The appearances that play with us in an action of transformative leisure are not tended to when we engage actions from a recreative mindset. For example, in tending to appearances in violin playing, I follow the dynamic markings and think about what it really means to be *pianissimo* as compared to *piano* as I consider how my part fits with the accompaniment if I am playing a solo piece or with the other orchestral voices if I am in a larger group setting. Recently, I've studied the orchestra suite by Gustav Holst, *The Planets*, in particular, *Mars*. In the opening of *Mars* the strings play a familiar repetitive rhythm of triplets, quarter notes, and eighth notes. The musical syntax indicates a bowing articulation that is uncommon in most orchestral and solo repertoire, *col legno*. This style of bowing requires that the wood part of the bow is used instead of the hair. The bow is turned by a movement of the wrist permitting the wood part of the bow to bounce on one of the strings of the instrument. This is a true percussive experience since the violin is played more like a drum than a typical string instrument. If I am playing *Mars* as recreation, I may be less likely to learn about *col legno* and adapt my regular bowing approach for this piece, especially if I do not understand why Holst wanted that particular sound.

In recreation, I may be less likely to acknowledge the appearance of this musical notation because it is easier to not learn how to play *col legno* correctly or it is simply accepted that I do not acknowledge the musical syntax as important. In transformative leisure, musical notations are just as important, and sometimes even more important, than the actual notes or pitches written. Transformative leisure implies a seriousness and depth of understanding that is not engaged or considered important when one does something from a recreative mindset. In recreation there is an acceptance of not acknowledging appearances.

As mentioned previously, in the experience of transformative leisure, one engages an *as-ness* that situates one inside an experience. In recreation, the experience remains within an *is* environment because *as-ness* is cultivated by tending to cointending, phenomenological attention, and appearances. *As-ness* tends to those kairotic moments that are engulfed within potentiality, possibilities, and serendipity. *If* environments are governed by a sense of chronos because the experiences are more likely breaks or moments of reprieve within one's every day demands.

Recreation is not bad. I not only play the violin for my leisure but I also engage recreation experiences that are fundamentally and phenomenologically different from my violin playing. For example, I read all of the Harry Potter books when they were first released. I also went to each Harry Potter film when it was released. I confess that I also attended several Hogwarts festivities at local book shops in celebration of the book releases. This was fun for me but it did not require a contemplative spirit and it wasn't hard work. My experience was governed by *chronos* in that I waited and measured time until the release of the book or film. I competed with myself and other friends reading as fast as I could so we could see who finished the book first. I scheduled my summer vacations around the release dates of the movies that were released in the summers. My experience with Harry Potter was driven primarily by *chronos*. I also did not prepare contemplatively for engagement of the books or the films. After I read one book, I did not think about the continuing story or contemplate the philosophical issues inherent in the narrative. I did not follow what the screen actors did in real life or the backstory behind J. K. Rowling, the author of the series, and her writing experiences. I did not work hard to prepare myself to read a book or watch a film; I simply enjoyed doing it for the moments of distance the activities gave me away from my own daily obligations and toil.

Reading Harry Potter stories and watching the respective films were recreative activities for me. My experiences with Harry Potter will not have the same impact upon my interiority as my violin playing. When I put a Harry Potter book down, I no longer think about it and when I left the movie theatre, I also left the story behind. In the spirit of recreation, I can talk to other people about the Potter narrative as memory permits. I can provide opinions on each character but I simply had a simple basic recreative experience that gave me pleasure for a short while until my own realities again confronted me with obligations in work and my personal life.

Transformative leisure is different for every person. I am not arguing that reading the Harry Potter series cannot be transformative leisure in fact, it can be for someone else. If one approaches the narrative, either in the books or the films (or both), in a contemplative spirit unbound by conventions and open to learning something new, reading Harry Potter stories can be transformative leisure. The key to experiencing transformative leisure is in one's approach to the phenomenon and being open to potentiality of the experience.

Another important phenomenological difference between transformative leisure and recreation is the transformative aspect that emerges without a seeking toward it. When I play my violin I become lost in the experience in such a way that liberates me from negative communicative structures. In other words, because I am inside the experience of violin playing, I have positive and constructive things to talk about with others that take the place of gossip or other hurtful communication patterns. Negative or hurtful communication patterns do not cultivate new ideas or advance older ideas. Negative or hurtful communication patterns can harm others and hold negative implications to your own self as well. Recreation may not focus on negativity but it does not habituate us to turn toward healthier communicative patterns either. In recreation we might develop some kind of new information to share with others but that information is not philosophically cultivated and it is still governed by time, competition, or other external outcomes which naturally involve limits and boundaries. Recreation does not liberate because the nature of recreative experience is itself limited and constrained.

There is one caveat to the general difference between transformative leisure and recreation phenomenologically and that is the idea that neither experience is final and unchangeable. By the very open nature of transformative leisure, this means it also cannot be totalized. Therefore, an experience of transformative leisure can change into an act or actions of recreation. The same is the case for recreation. In fact, we might begin with a recreative spirit but over time, that spirit might shift into a more contemplative action, which is necessary for transformative leisure. Likewise, there may come a time where transformative leisure shifts into a recreative experience due to unforeseen circumstances.

For example, I have had many stand partners in different orchestras through the years. I recall one violin player in particular that I shared a music stand with for several years. As I reflect upon her approach to orchestral playing, I consider her experience as more recreative in nature than philosophical. In regard to her experience at the time we were stand partners, she did not practice our music between rehearsals, she did not write up to date bowings or dynamic markings and changes in her music so that she could practice at home between rehearsals with the same markings as we shared in my music, which is what we performed from. When orchestra ended for the year, giving us three months off in the summers, she also never played during the summer. Her experience of violin playing was driven by chronos (a particular period of rehearsal dates and times, performing at concerts, and not giving other time to the play of the music). She told me she liked coming to rehearsals and having time away from work and home (especially her three children) where she could take a break from her daily demands and routine. Over the years her musical skill, sound, and commitment did not change—nothing serendipitous emerged in her playing and in her life; she experience no transformation up until the time I moved away. She experienced violin playing as recreation and it did serve a purpose but it wasn't transformative leisure because she did not engage the violin philosophically or phenomenologically. Playing violin for her did serve a purpose though. Today, all of that could have changed. Her recreative experience might have become less satisfying over time or her children could have grown up, leading her to crave a deeper and more cultivating musical experience. Today she could be experiencing her violin in a contemplative mindset and liberating herself all of the while. Her recreation could be transformed into transformative leisure.

It could also be the case for others that their experience of transformative leisure might shift into a recreative or work (employment) framework. For me, when I started to get paid for playing and I committed to playing for weddings on weekends, my transformative leisure shifted to work and I began to consider other things—my phenomenological focus of attention shifted to external things and away from the experience of playing the violin. As I made changes in my life, I began to shift back into a philosophically informed experience again only to lose my leisure once more with the death of my mother. When this occurred, no longer could I play my instrument at all. In fact, my philosophical spirit for living in general left me as well. It took years to regain my philosophical spirit but it did return. I now continue to experience transformative leisure through my violin, tending to the phenomenological aspects of playing and seeing where that might take me. The movement between transformative leisure and recreation is natural but it is necessary to know whether one is engaging transformative leisure or recreation because if we know this, then we will not deceive ourselves.

If I thought that my reading of Harry Potter, in the way that is described above, is an experience of transformative leisure, I would be in existential danger because thinking that one is engaging in transformative leisure when one is really engaging a recreative framework creates a false consciousness; it means I think I know more than I actually do know. This means that the cultivation experienced in transformative leisure cannot be experienced and one would not know the difference if her or she experienced it or not. One would be deceived into thinking that her or his interiority is something that it is not. This creates a "false consciousness" where one cannot truly know oneself or one's existential potential.

CONSEQUENCES: A FALSE CONSCIOUSNESS

Transformative leisure is concerned with absence as much as presence. In fact, without both, leisure reduces itself to something else. Without both absence and presence we risk becoming an *aleisure* society. Thorstein Veblen pointed to the notion of a "false consciousness" in his *Theory of the Leisure Class*.[23] What Veblen meant by a "false consciousness" is that human beings will be guided by crackpot realism if left unchecked. He made a distinction between Men of Affairs and Men of Decision (both two very banal compliments). Men of Affairs are men who were supposed to be sober and practical but in reality they were utopian capitalists and monomaniacs. Men of Decision are men that lead us to war and run our society but who are really crackpots who actually believe the garbage they sell the mass public. This creates an illusion or a false awareness that we have competent leaders and our affairs and decisions are in good hands. They weren't for Veblen. In fact, while Veblen was one of the most unruly critics of American capitalistic culture in the eighteenth century, he can also be hailed as a prophet because perhaps his concerns about leisure and the economy are just as relevant today.

A false consciousness for Veblen was tied to the notion of leisure in the sense that the leisure class he critiqued was only concerned with the outwardly presence and appearance of things while ignoring the absence of things. The presence and appearance of "things" that cost money and that create a visage of wealth, superiority, or privilege overpowered the acknowledgment of absence. Privileging absence balances presence but the negation of one over the other causes an imbalance which leads to the sense of having, owning, or experiencing something when one really does not have that experience. A false consciousness is dangerous in that it makes us think we are more than what we are or have more than what we have. Georg Lukács situates a false consciousness within the larger class consciousness. For him, a false consciousness results from a fossilized history of knowing as formalism renders human beings "incapable of comprehending" the real nature of things.[24] A false consciousness leaves human beings unable to be decisive as it creates a situation where there is persistent inflexibility to confront the true and false of things. When we lose what is now present and we see that there is nothing absent, we risk falling into an

---

23   Thorstein Veblen, *Theory of the Leisure Class* (New York, Mentor Books, 1953; 1899).

24   Georg Lukács, *History and Class Consciousness*, (Cambridge, MA: MIT Press, 1968).

abyss of narcissism that limits our ability to move forward in communicative space and time.[25]

If our communicative practices are guided by a false consciousness then how will we know what to take about in any given historical moment? Contexts will inevitably change and experiences will be driven by more than one competing good. If we do not know how to reflectively and opening engage ideas, how are we suppose to competently engage otherness in an age of difference? Transformative leisure brings to me a new vocabulary, an openness, an acuity to play with ideas that I do not otherwise have. In recreation I perform a task and I judge myself or others in that engagement. In transformative leisure I am concerned with my relationship with the thing that I am doing and I cultivate my aesthetic sensibilities by engaging for the sake of engaging and experiencing those moments without demand of something else. This agility permits me to be a competent and prepared communicator. Without this ability I succumb to a false consciousness if I do not recognize that transformative leisure and recreation are different.

In light of the leisure-recreation tension, a false consciousness is best exemplified when people of any class have too much opportunity to engage in recreative activities assuming that what they do is leisure. This is the self-deception, assuming that transformative leisure is recreation and there being no real distinction between the two terms or the actions. Additionally, it could be assumed that one's class permits the engagement of recreation activities to varying levels and this is true in some ways because if one is left to work-for-a-living, and live pay check by pay check, there are time constraints that physically limit the amount of time that one can engage non work related activities. This is a natural limit that acknowledges the time-measured limits on work days. However, we must find moments in our lives for transformative leisure so that work does not consume our time and our limits. A large quantity of time is required to make a difference because it is the quality of time that holds more meaning to the experience.

Consequently, a false consciousness reminds us that we must not permit absence or presence to overpower the other. We must balance presence and absence in our experiences so that we find a consciousness that permits human beings to grow in communicative space.

---

25   Christopher Lasch, *The Culture of Narcissism: American Life in an Age of Diminishing Expectations* (New York, Norton & Company, 1979).

Without this growth potential we risk becoming nothingness in an abyss of betweeness, we neither exist nor we do not exist.

CONCLUSION

This chapter has considered transformative leisure phenomenologically specifically related to action. By exploring phenomenological categories and providing phenomenological description of my own experience the essence of perception and experience helped us to understand the moments of transformative leisure as being different from action and experience in recreation.

Merleau-Ponty helped us to understand transformative leisure as a phenomenological experience governed by our perceptions. Merleau-Ponty's perspective provided insight into transformative leisure and action situated within the perceptual field of action. If we ask ourselves what makes transformative leisure so essential to human existence, we now understand that our perceptions inescapably link our actions.

Having this phenomenological understanding of transformative leisure should be a priority for all of us because if you engage more recreation than you do leisure, let me point you toward a more active participator status in your intellectual exercising. Keep recreative activities in your life but invite in the interplay of presence and absence of leisure into your experience as well. Be aware of this phenomenological interplay. This discussion has tried to shift our attention toward serious play by exploring the absence of presence and the presence of absence so that we can become more serious which has the potential to transform or reshape our next experiences – a "nexting" of sorts. Nexting refers to "doing something to keep the conversation going, responding to what's just happened, taking an additional step in the communication process." [26] Transformative leisure cultivates communicative ability to engage in nexting successfully as it prepares us to be competent communicators and genuine interlocutors. A way to consider the interplay of presence and absence can be illuminated in this quote from Algis Mickunas that focuses on Merleau-Ponty's phenomenology of the human body:

> When a friend calls me across the street and gestures for me to
> come over to look at some paintings in a shop, she begins to be

---

26 John Stewart, Bridges Not Walls: A Book About Interpersonal Communication (New York: McGraw-Hill, 2002), 33.

impatient by my delay, and her gestures, her bodily comportment, spread her impatience across my unwilling movements until finally I gesture my submission and go to look at the paintings. In short, we communicate through the oriented and kinesthetic space on whose background figures of our focus and attention emerge, to lift out figures in the phenomenal field with never a final say, never a final depiction of what these backgrounds and figures mean.[27]

Our attention goes immediately to appearances and we cointend meaning that is never full, never complete, and perhaps in a state of tentative knowing. This kind of approach provides room for growth and continued development of ideas and growth of relationships. This is an unknowing or less tangible aspect of knowing and it is uncomfortable to many who do not play in the realm of transformative leisure; bringing one to a defensive stance quite easily. Tending to transformative leisure prepares us to play in, negotiate with, and productively engage this tentative and sometimes contentious, communicative space. Now that I've already discussed transformative leisure in discourse and in action, the next natural step situates our focus on transformative leisure in community.

---

27   Algis Mickunas, "Maurice Merleau-Ponty: Communicative Practice" in *Perspectives on Philosophy of Communication*, ed. P. Arneson (West Lafayette, IN: Purdue University Press, 2007), 139-158.

CHAPTER 3

TRANSFORMATIVE LEISURE IN COMMUNITY

...in fact the realm of freedom actually begins where labour which is determined by necessity...ceases; thus in the very nature of things it lies beyond the sphere of actual material production...Freedom in this field can only consist in socialized man, the associated producers, rationally regulating their interchange with Nature, bringing it under their common control...and achieving this with the least expenditure of energy and under conditions most favorable to, and worthy of, their human nature. But it none the less remains a realm of necessity. Beyond it begins the development of human energy which is an end in itself, the true realm of freedom, which however, can blossom forth only with this realm of necessity as its basis. The shortening of the work week is its basic prerequisite.

−Karl Marx

The two stages through which the ever-recurrent cycle of biological life must pass, the stages of labor and consumption, may change their proportion even to the point where nearly all human :labor power" is spent consuming, with the concomitant serious social problem of leisure, that is, essentially the problem of how to provide enough opportunity for daily exhaustion to keep the capacity for consumption intact.

−Hannah Arendt

who is the other self that I encounter in my dealings with the world?

−Calvin O. Schrag

In chapter one I discuss transformative leisure in discourse and in chapter two I discuss transformative leisure in action which explored the phenomenological nature of the art of leisure in lived experience. Both of these environments help us to more wholly understand the experience of transformative leisure and its value to our human condition. This next chapter considers transformative leisure in community which takes us beyond looking at the self as a separate or disconnected entity. Communities are natural ontological structures that come into existence when multiple selves are living together sharing and forging their space interdependently. So, not only do they co-construct their space but they also are at once co-creating and constructing their relationships. The natural evolution from discourse to action to community comes from the intentionality and intelligibility of particular human actions which are the source of social practices that shape, govern and direct our lives.[1] In a community environment, communicative praxis becomes more and more important because mostly all of our actions are dependent upon someone or something else which constantly shape and reshape who we are and our future actions. I begin this discussion of transformative leisure and community with attention to work, labour, consumption and several other concepts that are revealed in our thoughts and actions within community.

There is an inescapable connection between labour, work, consumption, production, exploitation, alienation, and recreative fetishism. These metaphors are intertwined with transformative leisure from social, economic, or political philosophical perspectives, therefore, it is helpful to take a sociopolitical and economic look at the dimensions with which transformative leisure interrelates. The concept of alienation opens the discussion because it is significantly related to our interiority and it provides an opening that enables us to consider the socioeconomic realities that confront how leisure and recreation are experienced today.

Scholars confirm that Karl Marx had a theory of leisure in his sociopolitical standpoint that manifests through implicit negotiation of the metaphors of leisure and play.[2] As this chapter unfolds Marx's theory of leisure it becomes evident that the leisure he critiques in a capitalist society is what I argue is recreation in contemporary society. However, Marx does acknowledge that there is an activity consistent with transformative leisure and he describes this activity as a free manifestation of life that gives us enjoyment. This free manifestation is

---

1   Schrag, *The Self After Postmodernity.*

2   Laurence Hinman, "Marx's theory of play, leisure, and unalienated praxis," *Philosophy and Social Criticism* 5, (1978): 192-228; C. Rojek, "Did Marx have a theory of leisure?" *Leisure Studies* 3, (1984): 163-174.

further explicated by Laurence Hinman as *"unalienated praxis."* [3] The
metaphor of alienation is a descriptive way identifying the human condition without the experience of transformative leisure. The concept
of alienation is the consequence of capitalism and materialism.[4] Marx
believed that the productive man who accumulated wealth became
alienated from himself since wealth and excess is a barrier between the
human being and the ability to know one's self. This chapter considers
how socioeconomic aspects of work and labour lead us toward a consideration of the relationship between alienation and transformative
leisure. Additionally, the metaphors of consumption, production, and
exploitation help to explicate the notion of recreative fetishism in an
environment devoid of transformative leisure. Recreative fetishism is
representative of how contemporary society engages leisure or at least
what they think is leisure.

Karl Marx (1818-1883) began his career as a writer, journalist, and
editor. During his early career he became familiar with socialist and
communist ideas which contributed to his dedication to reforming industrial society. One of Marx's foci involved his quest to reform society
centering around his critique of capitalism. His writings are complex
as he writes in support of the working class in a pursuit to liberate
them from exploitation and alienation imposed upon them through
capitalist endeavors. An examination of transformative leisure should
consider socioeconomic matters informed by Marxist thought because Marx was philosophically concerned with the human condition
as it relates to labour and exploitation—two metaphors that are tied
to our understanding of alienation and that are inescapably embedded
in the community that shape the human condition.

ALIENATION

Karl Marx was not out to replace ideas with mindless action or change,
but wanted to fashion a practical philosophy which would help to
transform social and political structures. Marx understood that the
working class needed to be informed by a practical philosophy and
that the philosophy had to be meaningful in some way that made
sense to the working class narrative. In other words, Marx wanted to
make philosophy meaningful to common folks in such a way that it

---

3   Hinman, "Unalienated Praxis," 201.
4   Karl Marx, *Capital* Vol. 1 (New York: Penguin Books, 1990).

would sustain the value of *doing* philosophy as well as the nature of the human condition. By emphasizing philosophy, Marx demonstrated caution and thoughtfulness about his ideas and their consequences, especially when it came to his ideas about how people work together as a community.

Alienation refers to a *process* in which humanity loses something as basic, yet necessary, as its original innocence.[5] In other words alienation is a process as opposed to an outcome or a condition that is marred by a loss or rupture of one's humanness. Alienation is also a state of being for the worker in a capitalist society that is characterized by distortion, disillusionment, and frustration whereby the worker lacks an understanding that is sufficient to control her or his own social environment. The worker enters into an ontological condition that separates one from the labour of her or his own work.

In Marx's *Grundrisse*, a theoretically rich discussion of alienation is presented as a dissolution of all products and activities identified as having only exchange values which results in a dissolution of personal and social relations. This results in an alienation of things and objects from their producers situating human beings in a subordinate position to things or objects. In this practice, workers work but not for the product; there is an exchange where the product is transformed into the worker's subsistence but there is no personal or social relation attached to that exchange.

In a general sense, a condition of alienation has to do with a human being and her/his relationship to her/his own labour.[6] It points to a separation of something that is naturally connected to something else. Alienation indicates there is a separation of human beings from their own labour, which leads to a separation between human beings and their human essence or nature. For one to be alienated, one would not have control of her or his own work (labour) and is therefore, in an alienated relationship. This alienation negates any aspect of autonomy or any self actualization of the worker. The work becomes objectified and owned by the capitalist while it is disconnected from the essence of the worker. In other words, the worker does not own her or his own work since it is owned by the capitalist and the capitalist benefits from the labour of the worker over and over again. Therefore, the work produced becomes separated from the producer and this separation

5   Elster, *Karl Marx: A Reader* (New York: University of Cambridge, 1986).
6   Karl Marx, *Grundrisse* (Harmondsworth: Penguin Books.,1973).

alienates the worker from her/his fruits of labour and therefore from her or his human drive to make something for her or himself. In the process where human beings use instruments or tools to perform labour, there becomes an alteration between the human being and the object of labour. In this alteration the process extinguishes the product because the worker is alienated from her or his ownership/authorship of the labour. This means the outcome of labour alienates the worker's process of labour, negating any authorship entitled to the worker.

There are four types of alienation that represent Marx's concern related to capitalism. These types include the alienation between the worker and her/his human nature; the alienation between workers themselves; the alienation of the worker from her/his actual product or outcome of their work, and the alienation of the worker from the process of labour itself.[7] The first kind of alienation has already been stated and rests as, perhaps, the most serious kind of alienation to the human condition—a separation from one's essence. The second kind of alienation suggests that instead of the work acting as a connection or social relationship between the workers, it instead reduces their work to something to be traded and it becomes an economic artifact instead of a communicative action that brings human beings together.

The third kind of alienation is a separation between the worker and her/his product or outcome of the work done. In other words, and related to the first two types of alienation, since the capitalist actually owns the product and since the product becomes a commodity that is controlled by the capitalist, the worker becomes separated from the product of her/his own hands. The worker loses control of her/his own creation and this loss is an alienation that separates one from one's own work product. This kind of alienation can be like a woman giving birth and after the labour and birthing process her baby is removed from her hands and from her control—in this a physical rupture occurs. The fourth kind of alienation has already happened if the third kind of alienation has occurred. This is an alienation of the process of labour itself. Because the worker is not gaining anything from the outcome of her/his endeavor and because the worker has no control over the how, why, what, and where her/his work is done, there is an alienation of the process of labour that subsumes the worker. Once this occurs the worker is left engaging an activity that offers no

---

7   Ibid.

self-realization or potential for self-actualization.[8] The worker cannot transcend beyond alienated labour. This last kind of alienation represents a metaphysical rupture for the worker.

Once alienated from one's labour, the activity of the worker becomes mindless and perhaps scripted or patterned to ensure that the worker does not think for her or himself. This is perhaps the worst of all alienations as it renders a vibrant human being full of life and ideas to that of a robot-like "spexishness." [9] As a worker is alienated, she/he becomes spexish, a condition that marks the loss of rationality and desire which can ultimately lead human beings away from their essence and away from their ability to reason; away from their own awareness.

Each type of alienation is not separate and distinct from the other types. In fact, each kind of alienation is part of the other types and if one occurs it is most likely that all four kinds of alienation have or will occur, at once and be wholly experienced by the worker. This consummated experience is a serious alienation that has a permanent consequence to the worker's human condition. Ultimately, alienation has the potential to isolate the individual worker and remove the worker from her/his human potential and purpose for living. Alienation is a description of the human condition that leads to a perversion of individual and collective social and political values. One person should not own the labour of another person, nevertheless, this is natural and an organic outcome of capitalism. When one person owns the labour of another, they rent it, use it, wear it, and yet they never cultivate it. Capitalists take the labour of others and exploit it, wear it out, and discard it as if it is nothing of value after they are finished with it. While not always a positive concept, alienation offers insight into our discussion on transformative leisure since a life devoid of leisure also alienates the human being from her/his essence and human potential.

The idea behind transformative leisure is that it is an activity grounded in philosophical thinking that cultivates one's ability to communicatively negotiate the world in genuine ideas without negative or hurtful communicative action and with the ability to think outside of the box to move ideas to new and better realms. Philosophical thinking is not the type of activity one engages in during recreation, entertainment, or

---

8   Erich Fromm, *Marx's concept of man* (New York: Frederick Ungar Publishing Co, 1969).

9   Keith Stanovich, The Robot's Rebellion: Finding Meaning in the Age of Darwin (Chicago, IL: University of Chicago Press, 2004), 73.

relaxation activities. Philosophical thinking is hard work and contin-
uous. All of these types of activities, transformative leisure, recreation,
relaxation, etc., are needed for cultivation of our daily state of being,
but only transformative leisure can ensure against an alienation from
ourselves because it permits agents to tend to their own ideas, to play
with their ideas outside of constraints within a mindful and thoughtful manner, to have social relationships with others in the action of
transformative leisure, and to be a part of the leisure process itself.
Those who engage in transformative leisure are embedded within the
process, to the ideas, and to others in a genuine fashion. One way that
alienation occurs if one is engaging in recreation but thinking that
she/he is engaging in leisure. There is a self-deception in this kind
of alienation that can result in the failure of the person to be wholly engaged in ideas as owner, player, and shareholder of the process.
In a capitalist society it is hard to have the mind of a capitalist and
to engage leisure philosophically. One would need to be fully aware
of the distinction between leisure and recreation as well as be willing
to engage in a contrary fashion otherwise from capitalism—toward a
transformative leisure experience.

WORK, LABOUR, AND LEISURE:
A THEORY OF UNALIENATED PRAXIS

Laurence Hinman suggested that "unalienated praxis" closes the divide
between work and play.[10] In this activity, play and leisure are engaged
for their own sake while work is an activity engaged out of a need for
consumption. Scholars who identify a theory of leisure (or theory of
play) in Marx's writings concur that this theory is found in Marx's
critique of John Stuart Mill's *Elements of Political Economy* written in
1844.[11] Specifically, Hinman argues that "Marx provides the basis for
both a theory of the alienated character of play and leisure in capitalist society and an indication of the characteristics of unalienated play
and leisure."[12] In order to discover unalienated praxis, a discussion of
alienated play and leisure is helpful.

---

10   Hinman, "Unalienated Praxis," 201.

11   Laurence Hinman, "Marx's theory of play, leisure, and unalienated praxis," *Philosophy and Social Criticism* 5, (1978): 192-228; C. Rojek, "Did Marx
have a theory of leisure?" *Leisure Studies* 3, (1984): 163-174.

12   Hinman, "Unalienated Praxis," 193.

As the amount of free time increased for individuals in the industrial era, interesting consequences emerged. Instead of eliminating the problem of labour and alienation, increased free time reinforced and perpetuated alienation of labour by creating the following conditions. First, the condition in which someone would not have leisure when more factory work became available demanded time from people; second, the condition when leisure was justified only if the activity increased production; third, the condition when the worker had to give up money to engage leisure; fourth, the condition when leisure became dominated by private property and the desire to *have* overcame the desire of need; fifth, the condition when leisure is transformed into a pure act of consumption; sixth, the condition when leisure reinforced the alienation that work created; and finally, the condition when one engaged leisure to escape the homelessness and alienation of work.[13] The last two conditions are especially deceptive because when one viewed leisure as a primary source of freedom (a positive perspective) alienation from work could become equally amplified – there was no chance of a worker feeling at home at work. This kind of alienated leisure is a derivative phenomenon that has grown out of alienated labour. When leisure is only justified in terms of increased labour, production, or when it is sacrificed for money, transformative leisure becomes an illusion.

Unalienated praxis is a way of addressing the eclipse and illusion of leisure in a political and economic sense. Unalienated praxis is an activity embedded within a creative and free conditional environment that simply will change as a result of the liberation in time and experience. This experience holds intrinsic value to the actor. Alienated labour does not provide for intrinsic value and alienated leisure lacks extrinsic value. Unalienated praxis is productive, not of a physical thing, but connected with the idea of human life itself—the essence of what it means to Be. The idea of a human life is not a collection of everything that one accomplishes in her or his life but it means a human life as related to an ongoing creation of relationships. This kind of praxis is free, in that it is grounded in the essence of what it means to be human. We make choices to approach our activities in particular ways. Unalienated praxis tends to a practice of approaching something because we want to, not because we have a need to fulfill. Unalienated praxis is also a source of enjoyment and a way to share with other

13   Hinman, "Unalienated Praxis.

others in aesthetic play. This kind of sharing is a meditation that begins contemplatively but moves one to engage and act in public. The
contemplative aspect prepares one for the public engagement and a
public sharing with others. When one engages unalienated praxis, one
is not only close to one's self and others but one is also close to human
nature through a transcendence of consciousness. Unalienated praxis
is not only esoteric but also practical in that it is also connected to human needs, it provides one a place of home and ground upon which to
stand among others. In this transcendence and rootedness, one's imagination is developed. Imagination has been referred to as "the internal
dimension of all *praxis.*" [14] Unalienated praxis is ideally complex yet
it is multidimensional and not without its own problems. It could be
viewed as unrealistic, abstract, beyond the reach of human beings. Yet,
these ideas are clearly present in Marx's thought though they were not
systematically developed. Keeping this in mind, Marx still has much
to contribute to the discussion on transformative leisure.

The idea of work and labour or production and consumption and its
economic value is helpful to consider when exploring Marx's perspective on leisure and how he defines the term. Capital can be considered
a mode of production and "a *social relation between men* and things"
whereby the capitalist had exploitative power over human beings, so
much so that the capitalist could alienate them from themselves as
discussed earlier.[15] Marx would have wanted human beings to be liberated from the prison of material life as well as from religion, which
was created as a response to the alienation by the capitalist, yet it also
alienated the human being from her/himself.

Marx argued that:

> Capital presupposes that goods are not being produced for di-
> rect consumption by the producing communities, but are sold as
> commodities; that the total labour potential of society has become
> fragmented into private labours conducted independently of each
> other; that commodities therefore have a value; that this value is
> realized through exchange with a special commodity called money;
> that it can therefore start an independent process of circulation.[16]

---

14   J. Henroit, *Le Jue* (Paris: Presses Universitaires de France, 1969), 102.
15   Marx, *Capital*, 54.
16   Ibid., 54-55.

Labour in this passage indicates it is something that happens between a human being and nature. The use-value of labour is a couplet that means something comes out of the labour, such as a product that can be used by someone or something in a productive way. The product is not just an end result of labour but they are a necessary *condition* of labour. Therefore, the product must have a value and the more products made the more the value increases. The increase of value leads to the product becoming a commodity, which is the instrument for earning capital. The capitalist desires to earn more capital which is a key element in the alienation and exploitation of the common human being. Constraints related to the physical limits of the worker play a role in alienation too.

The work day is limited by the natural day which means there is an end to the day and this end is a constraint for the capitalist because work ends when the physical world says the day is over. Marx used an example of a horse that could only work physically for eight hours a day. So even though the day is twenty-four hours, the horse is limited to physical output for one third of the natural day, which is a natural constraint that limits production. There are also social constraints at play; those rules and obligations external to the individual that are imposed upon the worker. Social constraints include social expectations of work environments and expected social practices that impact the work day in some way. This relates back to alienation because of the amount of time working in the natural work day, the worker is alienated from social connections that can provide intellectual and social cultivation, especially when the natural workday perhaps subsumes one's ability to have social time. I've established the idea that human beings are alienated from themselves because of how work and labour are at odds in a capitalist society. So, the next question is, what is left for us as we think about community? What are we doing if we are not engaging leisure? One answer to this is simple, recreative fetishism.

RECREATIVE FETISHISM

Eliminating recreation or transformative leisure (one or the other) from the human experience would be a tragedy because we need both leisure and recreation to cultivate our interiority and provide rest from the toil of working for daily sustenance. Understanding the difference between the two, transformative leisure and recreation, would emancipate human beings and eliminate the opiate effect that occurs when the two experiences are considered as the same experience. This would dispel confusion and provide clarity that would give us a choice in our daily activities. On the other hand, if we do not recognize the distinction between transformative leisure and recreation we would be engaging Marx's idea of fetishism which is embodied in political and social parts of life that which includes consumption. In other words, we'd be engaging recreation as a fetish that shapes and controls our social life in which we over consume for the sake of the consumption itself. This overconsumption would subsume our political and economic life. A lack of understanding the distinction between transformative leisure and recreation contributes to the problem of recreative fetishism which also leads to alienation from the interior self and the human community. So, while the capitalist is the responsible agent of alienation in Marx's theory of capital, it becomes the worker her or himself who is responsible for her/his own alienation by recreative fetishism.

The interiority of human beings can be infected by alienation, estrangement, and separation by thinking that recreation and transformative leisure are the same kind of activity or action that generate the same consequences to the human agent. To know the difference between leisure and recreation, and then to be able to engage both at appropriate junctures in one's life, is a catalyst for emancipation from the exploitive nature and alienated condition of a recreation-only experience. The transformative leisure-recreation distinction is a precondition for living a philosophical life that illuminates awareness that both kinds of actions are valuable to human engagement.

Karl Marx advocated the emancipation of society as a whole from the accumulation of private property because this accumulation led to servitude of the common worker, a state of being whereby one is always in service to another which separates the individual from intellectual or social benefits of the action. Marx's call for an emancipation of the worker is a call for the emancipation of humanity as a whole. The type of exploitation that Marx argued against was a socioeconomic exploitation that cultivated a culture of fetishism and contributed to the exploitation, alienation, estrangement, and isolation of human beings from their own humanity, from other human beings, and from their own intellectual cultivation.

Marx's critique of capitalism and the division of labour contains within it an implicit theory of leisure that has yet to be fully excavated. Some scholars might suggest that since Marx really did not talk about *leisure* explicitly, there can be no real theory of leisure teased out of his thought, though others disagree.[17] A guiding principle in Marx's thought involves his perspective on human beings as agents born to live, work, and play in a community of others who do the same kinds of things, creating a system or narratival web of interactions that is shaped and governed by difference and arbitrary hierarchy. It would seem absurd to think that Marx did not consider leisure more than something trivial. The central tension in a capitalist society is a damaged sociability which confines people to roles, restrictive work, and other property relations. Working class relations present a depressing picture of the human condition as dehumanizing at best which estranges people from others and from the essence of what it means to be human. Some scholars suggest that Marx would argue people contribute to their own misery and permit themselves to be slaves and estranged from others.[18] But this is simply a symptom of a capitalist society. Perhaps in a socialist society transformative leisure could be productive and liberated from work since there is freedom in leisure; though that freedom is lost in a capitalist society.

Marx's perspective is not without its own flaws and contradictions, however, there is a good reason to include Marx's thought in the discussion pertaining to transformative leisure. The value is that it provides a philosophical starting place from which one can change thoughts and actions about the human experience from a socioeconomic position. We can think about transformative leisure over and over again (and we should) but without bringing it into a relationship with lived experiences from and between real people that discussion would be incomplete. Marx opens us to a real-world way to think about how transformative leisure works in an imperfect world of work. The work of Hannah Arendt also provides us with the same practical applications related to work, action, and labour.

Hannah Arendt's (1906-1975) social and political philosophies cover a vast range of conditions related to transformative leisure and relationships between human beings. I am most interested in her distinction between parvenu and pariah as well as her perspective on public, private, and social environments of interhuman engagement.

---

17   Laurence Hinman, "Marx's theory of play, leisure, and unalienated praxis," *Philosophy and Social Criticism* 5, (1978): 192-228; C. Rojek, "Did Marx have a theory of leisure?" *Leisure Studies* 3, (1984): 163-174.

18   Rojek, "Did Marx have a theory of leisure?"

Additionally, Arendt's consideration of work, labour, and action also continue the conversation. By first considering Hannah Arendt's 1963 noteworthy work, *Eichmann in Jerusalem*, I set our path starting out with a discussion of her metaphors *pariah* (and *conscious pariah*) and *parvenu* which becomes helpful as we unfold her other philosophies related to transformative leisure. After *Eichmann in Jerusalem* lays the groundwork for Arendt's political and social philosophy, Arendt's perspective on transformative leisure will be illuminated through the metaphors of work, action, and labour, as well as enlarged thought, so that we can consider more fully the significance of transformative leisure to the human condition. By turning us toward Arendt's work, I hope to show how transformative leisure is inherently political, and perhaps responds to Arendt's call to correct the past political and social mistakes by embracing *phronesis* and *praxis* in lived public action.

Arendt envisioned the public realm as interspaces that had the potential to embrace human plurality and create a vibrant public domain of human participants. She thought that this new space would be able to reach between the hearts of people and their ideologies in the spirit of respect, thereby, not dictating any particular or preferred way of engagement. But instead, what she saw was a dangerous political domain imbued with the illusionary aspects of liberation and political action. Arendt talked about transformative leisure and the spirit of the contemplative life as a way of preparing for one to engage in a plurality-imbued public sphere. Because of this contemplative spirit we can begin to engage ideas more deeply and constructively. Arendt wanted people to not only think philosophically and thoughtfully, but to also act upon those thoughts in an engagement with efficacy and authenticity toward the ideas and toward others. Arendt's controversial critique of *Eichmann in Jerusalem* opens the discussion.

ARENDT ON *EICHMANN IN JERUSALEM*

Hannah Arendt made particular and bold statements in her critique of Adolf Eichmann in *Eichmann in Jerusalem*. I begin with a general statement that Eichmann's actions took place within an environment not within a vacuum.[19] Additionally, she described Eichmann as a rational man who actually did not display a perspective of anti-Sem-

---

19   Hannah Arendt, *Eichmann in Jerusalem: A Report on the Banality of Evil* (New York: Penguin Books, 1963).

itism. Arendt suggested that Eichmann's actions were not of a man filled with hatred but of a man who was doing his job, his duty, and following the law of the land in which he was embedded. As a result of this, the examination and judgment of Eichmann's actions could not be complete without looking at the whole environment along with his individual actions. In the world's public consciousness, Eichmann had been touted as the author of the final solution that is responsible for concentration camps and other such atrocities that have given WWII a reputation laced with evil. Though, the idea that Eichmann was a scapegoat set up by the human community and dressed up in the devil's clothing would come to mar her ethos for some time to come. What she argued is that Eichmann was not really "evil" as religion defines evil as the devil. Rather, her conclusions about Eichmann were that he was a silly human being who gained power from the people's ignorance and that everyone perhaps has an Eichmann within them. She said that some people need a visual scapegoat and Eichmann was the scapegoat of the war but she suggested that the banality of evil is within all of us; not just in one person. She argued that we need to look at the person and his/her place in society to fully grasp the banality of evil.

Hannah Arendt drew several conclusions about Eichmann's testimony that more fully explain her perspective on Eichmann's impotence. She suggested that Eichmann was not the master of his own action and that at some point he failed to stand on his own ground only to stand on ground that was not his, rendering him impotent and unable to make his own judgments and take his own individualistic action. Arendt also suggested that it was evident that Eichmann could not think for himself as he reverted consistently to well prepped phrases that were either made up for his own defense or a simple collection of phrases that were general in nature and applicable to multiple circumstances. She said this characteristic is a type of "officialese" that actually made him appear communicatively challenged. In Arendt's explanation of the use of the term "officialese" she stated, "officialese became his language because he was genuinely incapable of uttering a single sentence that was not a cliché." [20]

Another conclusion that Arendt drew about Eichmann during his trial is her critique that he was a *joiner* of things and once he *joined* the SS his desire to join other groups as he had in the past was no longer an option for him. He had become a prisoner himself. Eichmann

20   Arendt, *Eichmann*, 48.

himself admitted he decision to join the SS was one that had a most uncertain and unknown future, "I sensed I would have to live a leaderless and difficult individual life, I would receive no directives from anybody, no orders and commands would any longer be issued to me, no pertinent ordinances would be there to consult – a life never known before lay before me."[21] Eichmann was not so much an intelligent person, in fact he was an individual who was not intelligent, who actually lacked the intelligence to commit some of the crimes that he admitted to committing. In this sense Eichmann was more of a braggart than a confessor which provided to him a cardinal vice because he actually feared failure and anonymity so much so that he would rather be executed as a war criminal than continue to live invisible to society.

Arendt's critique of Eichmann pointed to the idea that he and perhaps other Nazi criminals were actually not abnormal and not pathologically impaired. Instead, perhaps these were ordinary people who took any kind of action given their situation which actually rendered the actor powerless to make the right moral choices. Arendt's critique of Eichmann has had significant critique. Arendt has been criticized for not attending the complete trial as it is documented that she only attended the trial during the prosecution's case and perhaps had she attended the defense's case, her perspective might be a more complete picture. Nevertheless, Arendt made a good case in drawing conclusions about Eichmann's part in the Final Solution and her reputation would come to feel the brunt of her unique perspective.

Because people wanted a scapegoat upon which to blame the atrocities of WWII, this perspective was not accepted by the Jewish community in America or Israel and it is because of her interpretation of Eichmann's role in the Final Solution that Arendt fell out of favor with Israel and many peers in the academy. Arendt used her Eichmann conclusion to shape her critique of modern Jewishness. She would come to argue that Jews experienced catastrophic events during WWII that were not inevitable or accidental. She argued that the outcome resulted from a specific history of Jew-Gentile relationships. She found that Jews were so politically blind that they did not understand the implications and consequences of their own actions but she held her ground even when she knew that people did not understand her point. Because of standing her ground, she chose to accept whatever consequences would be forthcoming to her career and reputation. In the

21   Ibid., 32.

choosing of the role of a social outcast, or conscious pariah, she avoided the pitfalls that other Jews in Western Europe fell into.

The Jews who tried to separate themselves from their own Jewish tradition were never truly accepted by European society because they as they gained social glory they fell into political misery and if they gained political success they experienced social insult.[22] It is only recently, within the latter half of the twentieth century, that scholars began to more fully attend to Arendt's work and they have found that earlier public conclusions about her perspective were faulty. So there is a resurgence of interest in Arendt's philosophy and political theory that can be helpful to us today. Her work extends to exploring and critiquing labour, work, action, public, private, and social realms all related to the human condition and human interaction. Without Arendt's conscious choice to be an outcast (knowing that her opinion would be in disfavor), we might have lost some of the most significant philosophical and political work to emerge from a women in the twentieth century. She chose to take a public stand on her interpretation of Germany, Eichmann, and the events of the Final Solution. Arendt became a "self-conscious pariah" in the Jewish community because she made the moral choice to take a public stand that was intellectually supported while being dismissed by popular culture.[23] Hannah Arendt's understanding and application of pariah and parvenu become significant to our further discussion on transformative leisure.

THE PARIAH AND THE PARVENU

Arendt borrowed the perms "parvenu" and "pariah" from the French journalist and anarchist, Bernard Lazare.[24] Pariah is a word with a Sanskrit origin that indicates someone at the bottom of a caste system or perhaps someone outside of a caste system.[25] The pariah is an outsider and outcast who cannot and or will not erase their own fate of

---

22   Hannah Arendt, *The Jewish Writings* (New York: Schocken Books, 2007).

23   Seyla Benhabib, *The Reluctant Modernism of Hannah Arendt* (Walnut Creek, CA: AltaMira Press, 2000).

24   Bernard Lazare, *Jewish Nationalism*, trans. M. Abidor (LeNationalisme Juif., Paris: Stock, 1898); Bernard Lazare, *Antisemitism: Its history and Its Causes* (New York: Cosimo Classics, 2005).

25   S. Swift, *Hannah Arendt* (New York: Routledge, 2009).

difference.[26] In contrast, the parvenu denies that fatefulness and eras-
es her or his own difference by assimilating and negating difference
by adhering to the dominant trends or mores of any given culture.
By affirming Jewish particularity (and not assimilating into European
culture) pariahs became marginal in relation to European society and
to their own Jewish community. The conscious pariah is a hidden tradition of people isolated; those who willingly and intentionally accept
their exile, willing to remain within that public exile in their stance on
a principle or a condition. Again, for Arendt, the pariah is an outsider;
one who does not do well when society dictates taste, behavior, and
attitude for the masses. Arendt's pariah is one that is marginal and
borders on insanity at times while living with difference in a way that
highlights their difference in the larger society.[27] The pariah, the conscious pariah, is not afraid and is intentional in creating and accepting
her or his fate in society.

Arendt compared this outsider to that of the parvenu, those Jews
who tried to succeed in the world of the gentiles but could never
fully escape their Jewishness.[28] Parvenus seek out social recognition
through some kind of social acceptance into a particular group but
what they actually get really falls short of their desires because it is
a false acceptance—they are never fully accepted into that particular
group as an equal. The parvenus that tried to make it in non-Jewish
society are actually counterparts to Arendt's notion of pariah. Pariahs
use their minds and hearts but the parvenus use their elbows to raise
themselves above fellow Jews, at the cost of fellow Jews and their own
Jewishness, to move into a more *respectable* world of the gentiles. The
parvenus were only accepted in gentile society as an exception to the
stereotypical Jew in society. Parvenus think that they raise themselves
above pariahs and they pretend to fully exist and be accepted in a
world that they are not a part of but again, this acceptance is only as
an exception, they are never fully accepted.

In contrast, the pariah publically affirmed their Jewishness and chose
the public social exile as consequence of their affirmation in place of
selling out their tradition to a society that labeled them as subhuman.

---

26   Hannah Arendt, *Rachel Varnhagen: The Life of a Jewess*, ed. L. Weissberg,
       trans., R. Winston, C. Winston, (Baltimore, MD: Johns Hopkins
       University Press, 1997).

27   Benhabib, *The Reluctant Modernism.*

28   Arendt, *Rachel Varnhagen.*

Pariahs voluntarily spurn society's intention by being faithful to their own traditions. A pariah gains honesty and a worthy life as a consequence of their public isolation and exile for the "in" crowd. A pariah's view of reality is clear and it is clearer than that of a parvenu's view of reality. We can say that a pariah is one who stands their own ground no matter how out of favor that ground might become. The pariah is a better philosopher but parvenu fails to think for her or himself; the pariah has a gestalt sense of awareness but the parvenu is not aware of her or his inability to think and act upon one's own judgments. Keep the pariah-parvenu distinction in mind as I now discuss work, labour, and action as a bridge to transformative leisure.

WORK, LABOUR, AND ACTION IN COMMUNITY

To continue exploring transformative leisure and community, and in the spirit of Arendt's philosophies, her political theory provides a platform for discussion and critique on her ideas of work, action, and labour. In order to identify Arendt's perspective on transformative leisure it is helpful to understand how she defined these three aspects of her political theory. Additionally, it is helpful to consider her critique on Marx's definition of work and labour because they are contradictory in nature. Work is associated with activity that is unnatural to human existence because it is an activity that creates a second nature of something.[29] Work is required to build structures, monuments, and create cultural artifacts. Today, work would be considered making a film or writing a book. In contrast, labour is connected to a biological need or a basic condition of human existence. When we engage labour we are maintaining our biological existence in activities such as making breakfast, taking a shower, drinking water. Labour is an activity that is focused on maintaining our environment so that we can continue to live and breathe. In some ways, the first breath we take as a living human being is considered labour to Arendt. Work is inherent in consumption, unlike labour that which is inherent in a usefulness, though, labour can be transformed into work as boundaries can at times connect or overlap. Arendt provided an example of this transformation:

---

29   Hannah Arendt, *The Human Condition* (Chicago, IL: University of Chicago Press, 1998).

The most necessary and elementary labour of man, the tilling of the soil, seems to be a perfect example of labour transforming itself into work in the process, as it were. This seems so because tilling the soil, its close relation to the biological cycle and its utter dependence upon the larger cycle of nature notwithstanding, leaves some product behind which outlasts its own activity and forms a durable addition to the human artifice: the same task, performed year in and year out, will eventually transform the wilderness into cultivated land.[30]

In this example, Arendt argued that tilling the soil not only procures means of subsistence but it also prepares the earth for a long future and doing so, helps to shape and create the world as work would do. For a brief moment, let's consider how Arendt's notion of work and labour differ from Marx's understanding of the same ideas. Arendt critiqued Marx for blurring the boundaries between work and labour for he did not make a distinction between them. This is the key to Arendt's critique of Marx's political theory and her critique is considered one of the most significant critiques of Marx to come out of the twentieth century.[31] For Arendt, work creates a permanent world of objects and labour is the action that permits one to live in that habitat. The fact that Marx's did not make any distinction as Arendt made provides for a lack in his critique of production and consumption that would enable him to find value in leisure philosophically. While Marx does have a theory of leisure as we discussed previously, he could have made a stronger case, more explicit case, for leisure in his political theory had he made the distinction between work and labour.

Action, for Arendt, is an activity that occurs between human beings. Unlike work that creates our world and labour that is tied to our individual biological drives, action occurs between people and is connected to the human condition of plurality. People communicate through words and deeds. Human beings identify themselves and make themselves distinct from other human beings through words and deeds. From Arendt's perspective, human beings can live without Marx's labour as they can exploit people to do labour for them, such is consistent with his critique of capitalism. Additionally, human beings can live without work as wards of the state, never producing and

---

30   Ibid., 138.
31   Benhabib, *The Reluctant Modernism.*

contributing to the future of the world in which they live. But Arendt argued that human beings cannot live without action and without speech:

> A life without speech and action, on the other hand—and this is the only way of life that in earnest has renounced all appearance and all vanity in the biblical sense of the word—is literally dead to the world; it has ceased to be a human life because it is no longer lived among men.[32]

Arendt referred to action in speech and deed is the way in which we "insert ourselves into the human world."[33] So, action is how we mark the beginning of something new without which we would cease to be human. Arendt's understanding of action is more like a narratival action because action is embedded in an interconnected narratival space where

> The disclosure of the "who" through speech, and the setting of a new beginning through action, always fall into an already existing web where their immediate consequences can be felt. Together they start a new process which eventually emerges as the unique life story of the newcomer, affecting uniquely the life stories of all those with whom he comes into contact. It is because of this already existing web of human relationships, with its innumerable, conflicting wills and intentions, that action almost never achieves its purpose; but it is also because of this medium ... that it produces stories with or without intention ... in other words, the stories, the results of action and speech, reveal an agent, but this agent is not an author or producer. Somebody began it and is its subject in the twofold sense of the word, namely, its actor and sufferer, but nobody is its author.[34]

The action of speech and deed within a web of relationships and narratival action is the ingredient that gives life to the human condition. So far, Arendt's critique of Adolf Eichmann through her metaphors of pariah, parvenu and her distinctions between work, labour, action should be synthesized so that it points us toward the last metaphor of an *enlarged thought* in order to get to her perspective on transformative leisure. Beginning with her critique on Eichmann, we see that

---

32   Arendt, *The Human Condition*, 176.
33   Ibid.
34   Ibid., 184.

she is not providing excuses for him or his actions, lack of actions, or uninformed actions. Eichmann was a man who could not think for himself for a variety of reasons and he was not, in himself, embodied evil. It was his human condition that was uncultivated and unprepared to make moral choices because he was content with following orders and fulfilling his duty to the public, which for him was the German government. Eichmann was a caricature of a human being who has no real sense of self and conviction. This is much like playing a game that has become scripted through a set of rules or accepting the reality of being a spectator, either by failing to act at all or by acting in some kind of uninformed manner—just following orders perhaps. Anyone can follow orders but it takes a stronger person who uses forethought to engage ideas to go against the popular trend, such as is the actions of a pariah. One who engages in transformative leisure does so inten-tionally because the action begins with a contemplative approach to some thing situated in a freedom liberated from any intended out-come. A pariah is better able to engage transformative leisure because they choose to. A parvenu will not be open to transformative leisure if it is not the dominant trend at the given moment. Eichmann fol-lowed his orders and did his job well, though whether or not he took actions upon his own moral initiative is up for debate. The only prob-lem is that he did not take moral initiative in his choice. The parvenu wants acceptance at any price, regardless on the type of acceptance that results.

The distinction between pariah and parvenu enables us to see that transformative leisure cultivates the ground from which the pariah makes choices of engagement in the community; the pariah under-stands her or himself in relation to the world and bases decisions upon those respective positions. The parvenu is content with only engaging ideas if others think it is a good idea. Recreation does not require the commitment of the pariah to stand on particular ground but the par-venu *would* be content in recreation because the ground of recreation is differently structured. So, the pariah makes choices that sometimes require them to stand alone; a stance that isolates the individual from the community. Arendt's notion of action is an essential condition of the pariah, yet the parvenu stands outside of her understanding of action because the parvenu hides behind another doing their work and labour without taking individual ownership—the action is not a committed action, it is mere action. Arendt would find transformative leisure in the realm of action. From this elaboration it can be argued that the interiority of the pariah can be cultivated through transformative leisure, the experience of recreation does not contribute to that kind of cultivation. The cultivation I speak about comes from the idea of our enlarged mentality.

ENLARGED THOUGHT AND
TRANSFORMATIVE LEISURE

Hannah Arendt asserted the same distinction between transformative leisure and recreation as posited by this book. People have become separated from the leisure of antiquity.[35] She argued that the leisure of antiquity was not tied to consumption, as it is in her time and still today as evidenced by a healthy leisure industry in Western culture. Instead, she indicated that leisure is something consciously removed from all activities tied to consumption. So, with this acknowledgment and the understanding that her political and social philosophy was heavily influenced by Greek culture and philosophy, Arendt situated leisure as a philosophical undertaking which we can tie to her notion of enlarged thought.

Arendt vacillated between aspects of Aristotelian judgment and Kantian notion of universal moral principles as she considered the idea of enlarged thinking or an enlarged mentality, a term she borrowed from Kant. Enlarged mentality refers to the capability of one's thinking/thought quality of judgment that enables one to comprehend multiple narratival perspectives. Enlarged mentality is an important principle in the public-political realm but Arendt believed that the Platonic model of the soul and the unity of its parts were also essential for public-political action, a perspective that resonates with the ancient ideal that leisure cultivates one' soul. Enlarged thinking contributes to the human potential by considering issues of plurality in ways that otherwise are not visible. Arendt pointed to, though never fully unpacked, the idea that enlarged mentality or enlarged thinking is not grounded in the capacity of empathy but instead it signifies a cognitive ability to think with others and to see their perspective even if it opposes your own perspective. This ability to think perspectivally implies an autonomy of one's inner world while appreciating the standpoint of others and without distorting it.

---

35   Arendt, *The Human Condition.*

The acceptance of an enlarged mentality or thought is cultivated by the action of transformative leisure because a precondition of doing leisure is the ability to be open to new ideas and perspectives as well as embracing the serendipitous that might emerge in the experience. In short, while not fully elaborating a leisure theory in her social and political theory, Hannah Arendt offers the preconditions that are necessary for transformative leisure and its transformative potential. Action and an enlarged mentality are preconditions for the conscious pariah, and it is likely that a pariah will be attracted to transformative leisure and the parvenu will be attracted to recreation solely on the basis that everyone else is doing it. In her social and political theory there is a place for transformative leisure to cultivate one's ability to engage others with productive and constructive ideas and for one to be open to plurality of perspectives while embracing difference and standing one's own ground.

CONCLUSION

In thinking about transformative leisure and what it means to the communicative being and within the community, we cannot escape social, political, and economic aspects that inform, challenge, and constitute the experience of leisure in everyday practice. Both Marx and Arendt help us see the sociopolitical advantages to living a life full of transformative leisure. Hannah Arendt certainly had ideas related to leisure that were inescapably tied to her political and social thoughts as well as her critique of the conditions that created the Final Solution. How we communicatively exist is a choice embedded within historical conditions that are tied to philosophical, social, political, and moral precepts that need to be identified/acknowledged in order to move forward and embrace the next moments in our experience and histories. While the metaphor of choice can be considered an illusion due to social, political, economic constraints, we cannot know our human communicative condition without seeking out an understanding that is independent from our embeddedness. Transformative leisure is a radical philosophy that has the potential to create a society of genuine and intellectually generous citizens driven by an aesthetic impulse rather than an impulse immersed in production/consumption, work/labour, and exploitation/alienation. Transformative leisure helps us to intellectually negotiate our experiences and embeddedness that can inform how we take public political and social action. As we have moved from transformative leisure in discourse, in action, and now in community, it seems a natural evolution to consider is transformative leisure in transcendence—seeking ethicality, potential and the unknown.

CHAPTER 4

TRANSFORMATIVE LEISURE IN TRANSCENDENCE

What we find is a concern with alienation or estrangement and the necessity of working to overcome it

—Ramsey Eric Ramsey and David James Miller

From within the hermeneutical circle so understood, ethos is envisioned as a way of saying human being is always a dwelling; it describes our embodied being-in-the-world and our lived embodiment of world and words, not simply our character

—Ramsey Eric Ramsey

The correlation between knowledge, understood as disinterested contemplation, and being, is according to our philosophical tradition, the very site of intelligibility, the occurrence of meaning (sens). The comprehension of being — the semantics of this verb — would thus be the very possibility of or the occasion for wisdom and the wise and, as such, is first philosophy.

—Emmanuel Levinas

Spiritual exercises are required for the healing of the soul.

—Pierre Hadot

Transformative leisure transcends self, other, and community. Transcendence of self begins with alterity though it might at first seem like a contradictory starting place. As discussed previously, transformative leisure begins in a contemplative spirit that cultivates a spirit of selflessness recognizing first and foremost the other. Because this recognition begins with the other, we experience transformative leisure through alterity. Emmanuel Levinas (1906-1995) tells us that the other holds us in demand, not so much by the physicality of the person, but it is the metaphysical trace or echo of the other that holds us to an ethical apriori response. This chapter seeks the transcendence in transformative leisure through two different ethical lenses. The first is the ethical lens of Emanuel Levinas who advocated we are our brother's keeper as a first principle. The second ethical lens situates transformative leisure as a virtue ethic from the philosophy of Josef Pieper who was already an advocate of transformative leisure. This argument extends Pieper's treatise on leisure by explicitly connecting his virtue ethic philosophy to his philosophy of leisure—something he did not explicitly argue yet the threads are naturally woven together in this chapter. Transformative leisure cultivates our interiority that responds to the revelatory call from the other creating an existential rupture of our agency. If we do not attend to that demand we turn away from the other causing an existential disruption, much like a rec-reative condition that might replace our experience of leisure. Josef Pieper pointed to the idea of transformative leisure as a virtue ethic implicitly in his discussions involving virtues of the human heart re-lated to silence; happiness and contemplation, where he explores the *vita contemplativa* more explicitly; the concept of sin as a pathway to transformation; the fortitude that human beings must embrace and experience to survive the end of history; and his reflection on tradition and the philosophical act. We have an ethical obligation to nurture our communicative Being because that is the mode through which we engage Otherness, and we nurture our communicative Being through transformative leisure. This discussion begins by illuminating the sig-nificance of alterity in our lives which provides insight into transfor-mative leisure in transcendence and what transcendence means to the human condition.

ALTERITY: THE OTHER

Alterity is central to our interhuman experience as it transcends our relations with others. Extreme directness or peering into the face of the other brings upon our individual death of sorts because of the di-rectness that we realize we exist because of the other; we do not exist because of our individuality. Emmanuel Levinas explained:

> Responsibility deriving from no guilt; a gratuitous responsibility
> responding to a commandment not to leave the other alone is his
> or her last extremity, as if the death of the other, before being my
> death, concerned me; as if in that death – invisible to the other who
> is exposed to it – I became by my indifference the accomplice while
> I could do something about it.[1]

This means that our responsibility for the other is never-ending; we are never released from it. Even if we are not competent in our communicative abilities to act on our responsibility, the idea that our responsibility is never removed from us, changes how we see the world around us and calls us to engage in an ethical framework and placing priority of our communicative ability above other desires.

The idea of the infinite is situated within the idea that the I is more than itself. In other words, there is a surplus in the relationship with the other, it is a social relationship, not in a worldly sense and not in the sense that Hannah Arendt gives to the term *social*. Rather, the social relationship to which Levinas refers consists of the approachment toward an absolutely exterior being. In this approaching of the other, there is a learning experience that is only made possible by the otherness of the experience. In this social relationship the I is in the presence of the face of the other with a "total uncoveredness and nakedness of defenseless eyes . . . a disquietude of consciousness, seeing itself, in all its adventures, a captive of itself [. . . and] forbids me my conquest."[2] This relationship has an ethical resistance within this infinite space and we are at once charged with a responsibility toward that other. In this infinite relationship we realize that the infinite is not the object of contemplation but contemplation resides in the infinite. Understanding communicative space as a social relationship helps to distinguish leisure from recreation in that contemplation in transformative leisure resides in the idea of the infinite but that in recreation our attentions reside in the object, which is totality.

Desire permeates alterity but it is unquenchable because it does not need food; the insatiability rests in the cognizance of alterity. In desire we become open to being and at the same time we are disinterested

---

1   Emmanuel Levinas, *Alterity & Transcendence*, trans. M. B. Smith (New
     York: Columbia University Press, 1999), 127.
2   Emmanuel Levinas, "Philosophy and the Idea of the Infinite," in An
     Introduction to the Philosophy of Emmanuel Levinas, trans. A. Peperzak
     (West Lafayette, IN: Purdue University Press, 1993), 110.

turn away from ourselves. This desire is not a worldly love but rather it is the exercise of moral exigency which can only occur in our disinterestedness, our turn away from agency. This is where our moral conscience exposes our freedom in judgment toward the other. This moral conscience of pure desire cannot exist in totality but only in transcendence toward the other. Morality is not particular because it transcends worldliness toward a metaphysical first philosophy. So, an authentic disinterestedness toward the other is an *apriori* responsibility that human beings reach through transcending separateness by reaching toward and beyond the exteriority and interiority of alterity. In other words, according to Levinas,

> [a]n openness of the self to the other, which is not a conditioning or a foundation of oneself in some principle . . .but a relation wholly different from the occupation of a site, a building, or a settling oneself . . .reveals all its meaning only in the relationship with the other, in the proximity of a neighbor which is responsibility for him, substitution for him . . . it is disinterestedness, excluded middle of essence, besides being and non-being.[3]

This is the a human ethical apriori that guides Levinas's first philosophy in which we lose ourselves in the Other, in otherness that transcends toward alterity and privileges the relationship and not the I. It is the I and the neighbor that attends to this responsibility beyond worldly agency and totality. But this isn't easy for human beings situated within totality. The notion of inner discourse enables the I to understand its own situatedness and it is the habituation of this inner discourse that permits the I to turn toward the face of the Other in an infinite consciousness and meet alterity in its own interiority. Our relationship with alterity ensures proximity as a responsibility for the other as the I becomes hostage to the other in a consummation that permits death and transcendence at-once-and-already.

The notion of alterity and otherness is an apriori anchor within Levinas's notion of responsibility which situates the responsibility of the I for the Other as a first philosophy setting forth the groundwork for consideration of transformative leisure as an ethical paradigm from which one engages the other.

---

3   Emmanuel Levinas, *Totality and Infinity*, 181.

RESPONSIBILITY

Language comes with strings attached; it is born embedded in responsibility. In our seeking of the other we are already creating a relationship and responsible for that relationship to and with the other. It is through that responsibility toward the other, without a reciprocal demand, that the "I" or the "We" becomes possible. In this case, individuals are derivative essences of the other and we are derived without demand toward the other. The uniqueness of this derivation is that Levinas counters the assumption and privilege of agency with an ethic that begins with answering the call of the other and in this response, the I becomes.

There is an inconvenient understanding that has a tendency to shake the very foundation of individualism and existence in western culture which is the notion that human life is a phenomenological call to attend to the other, which diminishes the "I" and the "me" culture that drives politics, the economy, entertainment, and education today.[4] So, we are not here for ourselves; we are here for the other. In fact, as a totally embedded agent within western culture negotiating self will and desires, one might respond to this alternative in a defensive manner because it is totally foreign to think of one's self as derivative of another's existence. But this is not quite accurate. It is not that the I is derivative of the other in existence but the I is derivative in its *response* to the Other. We exist with the other when we respond toward the other. The I finds its identity when responding to the Other. The paradox that Levinas reveals is that without caring for the Other, one "puts one's own identity at stake."[5] So, in order to find one's self, one must respond to the Other first in order to become one's self in that response.

The consequences of failing to respond or failing to answer the call of the Other is consistent with the notion of a false consciousness that was discussed earlier pertaining to mixing metaphors of leisure and recreation. For Levinas, if we fail to respond to the call of the Other because of the western notions embedded within western culture of self-derived origins of the self, we engage in what Nietzsche described as a form of bad conscience. A bad conscience hides truths and creates an illusion that impedes one's ability to engage the Other authentically

---

4   Arnett, "The Responsive 'I.'"

5   Ibid., 40.

and ethically.[6] As we see from the consequences set forth in the post-modern era, and presupposing that the modern era was grounded on the illusion of progress, engaging others through a bad conscience has had quite the negative and morbid consequences that ushered in a re-velatory call to recognize the modern world had ended and a new, very different postmodern world had emerged.

Levinas stated that this "inescapable and nontransferable" turnabout from an "every man for himself" attitude into a priority of the "for-the-other" can only happen in a responsibility for the Other where there is a "radical turnabout . . .an encounter with the face of the other."[7] In this turn to the face of the Other there is an interior dialogue, an inner dis-course that becomes an interdiscourse. This is where the connection of transformative leisure to Levinas's philosophy becomes explicit. In transformative leisure one engages in contemplative and serious play. This serious play begins and occurs within an inner discourse. This is a practice or habit of sorts that permits an interdiscourse of serious play to emerge between the I and the Other in which the interdiscourse can then be seen as life giving because it is through the interdiscourse, the response to the Other that the I is derived.

Responsibility is inescapable in that one can never hide from it or from the other which is often the challenge we face. This is a difficult freedom in that it is an odd and uncomfortable privilege that imposes inequality and obligation on others who cannot be demanded upon in return. In other words, the responsibility we have toward an other is one-sided and our own burden yet it is difficult in the sense that we cannot demand this of the other in reciprocity, we must let the other free to not share our burden.

DIFFICULT FREEDOM

The freedom of knowledge is inspiration for the mind. Knowing (contemplation or knowledge) is a concept of consciousness in which one is conscious of something that is inseparable from an object. In this knowing there is tension that negotiates intellectual activity that seizes something to make it your own something. Knowing reduces a

---

6   Friedrich Nietzsche, *On the Genealogy of Morals and Ecco Homo* (New York: Vintage Books, 1967).

7   Levinas, *Entre Nous*, 202.

presence to a representation which appropriates and grasps the otherness of something known.

Difficult freedom involves aspects of guilt and innocence of being.
In the tensions of guilt and innocence, with regard to the other, there
is a totality of being that presupposes that if I am free, then I am totally separate from the whole of my being, which is the other. In this
separation, totality always remains incomplete. The difficult freedom
held within these tensions of guilt and innocence is that one's actions
always effect the other in the freedom between the I and the other.
The difficulty remains that the I is always in the presence or the face
of the other.

As an interlocutor, he faces me; and properly speaking, only the interlocutor can face

> without "facing" meaning hostility or friendship. The face as a
> de-sensibilization, as de-materialization of the sense datum, com-
> pletes the still encumbered movement in the figures of mythologi-
> cal monsters in which the body, or the animal half-body, allows the
> evanescent expression on the face of the human head they bear to
> break through.[8]

The difficulty of having freedom in our communicative relationships
with the other rests in the idea that the I has the potential for violence
and nonviolence in our relationship between self and other. To embrace this relationship and responsibility ethically one needs to begin
with a thoughtful, well-thought out, disinterested action toward the
other.

Emmanuel Levinas's project entitled, *Difficult Freedom*, contains numerous essays that explore Judaism, politics, aesthetics, ethics (first
philosophy), and critiques of other philosophies of the interhuman
experience.[9] Understanding that *Difficult Freedom* was written in the
aftermath of World War II and specifically influenced by the actions
within the Holocaust, these essays come together and ask questions
about the place of Judaism in the world, the effects that were to come
from Hitler's exterminations, as well as other related questions pertaining to Jewish spiritualism and political theories related to Israel
and Jewish education. Interpreting what Levinas means by his met-

---

8   Ibid., 33.

9   Emmanuel Levinas, *Difficult Freedom: Essays on Judaism* (Baltimore,
     MD: Johns Hopkins University Press, 1963).

aphor of *difficult freedom* has its challenges but nevertheless it can be done and conceptually applied to the transcendence in the doing of transformative leisure as well.

In Levinas's discussion of antihumanism and education, he admitted that one response to the recovery of humanity (in the aftermath of World War II) is to turn back toward Jewish education and Jewish teaching in general to a tradition steeped in conservation and morality. This response is a freedom of choice that involves difficult considerations, since what he suggests is that the healing of the Jewish people can be achieved though the State of Israel and turning toward the particularism of Judaism. For Levinas, Jewish education did not rely on brutal impositions in order to maintain educational freedom. Rather, Jewish education engaged ideas and practices that safeguarded the human in human beings. Levinas reminded us that we must live within the historical moment while continuing to repair and heal in a forward motion, the difficult freedom of maintaining a difficult past in one's memory and in one's proximity:

> The expressing of the face is language. The other is the first intelligible. But the infinite in the face does not appear as a representation. It brings into question my freedom, which is discovered to be murderous and usurpatory. But this discovery is not a derivation of *self-knowledge*. It is heteronomy through and through. In front of the face, I always demand more of myself, the more I respond to it, the more the demands grow. This movement if more fundamental than the freedom of self- representation. Ethical consciousness is not, in effect a particularly commendable variety of consciousness.[10]

Here, Levinas exemplifies the metaphor of difficult freedom as having taken ourselves hostage in this first philosophy of responding to the call of the other, in the face of the other. It is through this response that we are required to respond. The more we respond, the more likely we respond further, in depth, without question, and in genuine response. While we are free in our humanity, we are never free, since we are inescapably tied to and link with the other as a hostage to her/his guest. This welcome is a difficult freedom in that it is an undeclinable and inescapable responsibility. As an example, Levinas states that the difficult freedom for Jews is that they are chosen and the chosenness is a responsibility that cannot be avoided which involves a kind of

---

10   Ibid., 294.

tolerance for difference and alterity. We are at once welcoming and at once become a hostage to the other in the uttering of that welcome. It is in this relationship, and only this relationship, that the I can transcend and become a self, in the response to the other, for-the-other. This relation that the I has with the other is apriori, and comes with a necessary violence that encroaches on the sovereignty of the other. With this same kind of inescapability, transformative leisure lays out a path of transcendence for our human condition.

ETHICAL TRANSCENDENCE OF ALTERITY

It is helpful to follow Levinas's notion of first philosophy or the most fundamentally transcendent aspect of humanity, toward an idea of what transformative leisure look like in transcendence. Beginning with the presupposition that the ethical relation between human beings is the foundation of all knowledge and experience, transformative leisure holds us accountable to the other. When we are thinking agents in the world we are in a condition of confusion and we can no longer focus on what we should think about. But it is when we are engaged, as opposed to thinking, that we become alive in the world because in that engagement we lose ourselves, our interestedness, and turn toward the other in a disinterestedness of the self as we embrace or engage the otherness that fully situates us in the world. This notion of engagement is the play of transformative leisure; when we are fully at play in a disinterestedness that is when we are more fully alive in the other. Transformative leisure provides the cultivated ground from which we engage the other, leading us toward a transcendence that reveals the self and the other as one.

Privileging alterity encapsulates transformative leisure in the realm of doing so that we ensure our ability to begin with the other and turn away from self will and agency. Emmanuel Levinas's philosophy provides one way of exploring the import of transformative leisure to the human condition that presupposes an inescapable responsibility toward the other. Transformative leisure cultivates our ability to sober up and shift our focus of attention toward the other within a disinterestedness in seeking transcendence. Human beings cannot find the infinite within a worldly realm of agency nor can human beings transcend in the dimension of humanity and the other because we are drunk in ourselves and for ourselves. This is not a futile condition as human beings are capable of sobering up and of attaining this disinterestedness and the energy it takes to ethically engage toward the other. The condition of interestedness or agency is embedded within a nonreflective consciousness, a consciousness without a pre-reflective condition, but by embracing our responsibility toward the Other human beings can transcend this condition moving toward a condition of disinterestedness that transcends conditions of totality.

Transformative leisure moves one toward a metaphysical desire of infinity because one is removed from those conditions of totality. Transformative leisure helps one to transcend a muddied human condition into infinity. The link between Levinas's philosophy of self and other and transformative leisure originates in the notion of play. Levinas turns back toward a traditional understanding of discourse to define his understanding of inner discourse, which is when the mind is in a synchronic presence despite a *to and fro* movement that does not need to conform or become a consensus. This means that unity and presence co-exist in the worldly reality of inter-human communication. In this, the I enters into the thinking or thought of the Other, there is an interiority in this communicative mode. The ability to enter into this interiority is cultivated in the habituation of transformative leisure in one's life that remains fully separate from the empirical world by residing in the inner discourse action that shapes the *poiesis* in the experience of transformative leisure.

Within this inner discourse there is an exchange of ideas, an intellectual activity that creates a presence or a representation of something else which cultivates a field of knowledge that can be applied to a gathering of the betweenness of the self and other or of gathering alterity into the presence of the I. In this space we are disinterested in ourselves and interested toward the otherness of the other, driven by ideas and not by the totality of being. Engaging otherness in this way is not a common practice in a world driven by impressions, facades, and a chronological temporality, so we must learn how to find this space of engagement and then cultivate our ability to engage inner discourse so that we may be able to transcend the totalizing aspects of the world and move toward an experience of infinity. We must continue to seek and explore the idea of what it means to exist in relation to the self and other together. Transformative leisure calls out to us through a revelatory trace to explore our existence in transcendence.

Our communicative lives are confronted by competing and ever-changing technologies, social and political unrests, environmental uncertainties, questions pertaining to faith and existence, and at this juncture in world history, popular culture obsessions in media with an approaching apocalyptic prophecy. How do we then move beyond these competing and confrontational narratives? A brief note on each of these aspects of our lives can helpful in pointing us toward transcendence. Competing and ever-changing technologies are revealed through social networking sites, relationship development sites, the ability to carry instant music around with us and access it with the touch of a button, telephones that are now computers and computers that provide telephone service, electronic calendars that can fit our lifetime into the palm of our hands, and so on. There is seemingly no limit to the development and advancement of technologies that pervade our everyday lives. No matter how much one resists the temptation to enter into a relationship with technology, it will get us, drawing us in as if we have no human will left to act as our conscience and consequently rendering us incapable of making decisions within an enlarged mentality that cannot be captured or harnessed in a micro chip. The wide range of technologies that are invented to bring human communicative beings closer together are more likely to become a barrier that keeps human beings from communicating with each other in a truly human sense. Martin Heidegger felt that communicating through talk was fundamentally human and an activity in which people experience that notion of *being with* another. When we begin to communicate through virtual and cyberspaces something fundamentally changes with the notion of *being with* and this experience might well be the beginning of the end of *being with* in general.

The next aspect to consider is that of social and political unrest. At the time of this writing, The United States is experiencing social and political unrest exemplified by our military presence in the Middle East and nervous tensions amid North Korean rhetoric over nuclear missile testing. Many other countries are in some kind of military conflict as well. It might well be said that much of the world is in either war or serious conflict in some fashion or another. Headline news reminds us of the realities of genocide, human rights violations, public political downfalls, competing perspectives on social issues that fail to acknowledge and respect opposing perspectives, corporate irresponsibility, and a general mistrust of the prevailing social and political leaderships that govern the United States and other cultures around the world. These are all examples that fail to find common ground with the other which would, if we did find common ground, enable embracing the interhuman—our existence with the other. The failure to identify and accept the precipitating cause of crises and the burden of our emotional future, the future of our families, and the health of our general livelihood as a human race is all at stake. The contingencies of one country's financial market necessarily impacts economic conditions of other countries; the domestic real estate market has global implications, and the domestic unemployment rate affects every other area of our culture and our relationships with other cultures. All of this indicates that we, as human communicative beings are interconnected with other living communicative beings no matter where one is existentially located.

The third aspect involves environmental uncertainties that confront our natural resources, and therefore, the fate of the human race. Whether concerns arise regarding the April 2010 BP oil spill crisis that has catastrophic implications to our natural resources, plant life, animal/marine life; the March 2011 earthquake/tsunami/nuclear meltdown in Japan; the global warming argument that has the scientific community divided in areas of either argument legitimacy or potential consequences and responses to the condition; or questions of sustainability related to human consumption, it is certain that our global environment cannot remain the same and may not always be productive in such a way that supports forms of life. In other words, we simply cannot take existence for granted. We must find ways of ensuring that we do not over consume ourselves into oblivion. Part of this responsibility is to be aware of our consumption practices and conditions so that we are able to be thoughtful about how we engage the world as a collective community of communicative beings. Understanding how we are "being with" other communicative beings can help us to negotiate these contingencies otherwise than in a vacuum. The next aspect concerns questions of faith and existence. When we are not in a vacuum, questions pertaining of faith and existence confront us daily. In contemporary society, our faith is challenged through easy access to competing paradigms. An historical examination of the history of faith reveals multiplicities of faiths that have either endured or expired throughout history. Especially at times of great challenge or change, questions of faith and existence permeate human consciousness in ways that reveal realities of the unknown. This kind of awareness can either bring the human communicative being to new understandings or resituate one into a state of collective narcissism. Questions of faith and existence are not necessarily a negative thing for human beings yet if all one has is situated within a questioning, there is no end and no rest. In some ways, the rise of new age discourse and spiritualism to-day exemplifies the propagation of questioning that mirrors the myth of Sisyphus, never ending and never resting—a plight for human exis-tence in a contentious world.

Finally, the last aspect that signifies an imposition of competing par-adigms is the overrepresentation in popular culture of an apocalyptic obsession. We have surpassed the year 2012 in which many cultural myths propel an apocalyptic vision that is told and retold through vari-ous forms of media.[11] Some of these visions include end-time religious ideologies and natural catastrophic disasters—and a variety of end-time dates emerge to confuse us even more. Popular culture media representations of apocalyptic visions bombard our radio (broadcast and satellite), television (broadcast, cable, satellite), cinema, and most proportionately, the Internet. There is a multicultural preoccupation with end-time prophetic visions that is inescapable to the human com-municative being and this creates a sense of loneliness, homelessness, and the need for escape into a less reflective existence; a way of deny-ing the realities that bombard our questions pertaining to connections with the others and our lives as we make them. Popular culture is not the venue that recognizes these uncertainties. The academy has a sim-ilar perspective.

It is in the academy where we find philosophical perspectives that help us to understand the nature and need for transformative leisure in our lives. Scholars and philosophers pursue questions that con-sider how we, as human communicative beings, come to understand how transformative leisure can help us to negotiate contingencies that threaten our human existence. For example, a phenomenological see-ing has the potential to enable us to see beyond these uncertainties and contingencies that confront us. This kind of seeing beyondness can recuperate our communicative condition which nurtures our com-municative beingness. It is our communicative condition that is at risk because it is through communication that we embrace our humani-ty—in the-living-with-others.

---

11   Annette M. Holba, K. R. Hart, "Introduction." In Media and the Apocalypse, eds. K. R. Hart, A. M. Holba (New York: Peter Lang, 2009).

Martin Buber sought the interhuman experience. We experience the interhuman through our relationships with others—unimpeded by uncertainties, contingencies, changing technologies, fear of the unknown, and so forth. Understandably, transformative leisure helps us to see the world through an interplay of presence and absence in our relationships. Intentionality also helps us understand how and why we shift our phenomenological focus of attention toward something other than the self—toward the interhuman. The idea of a phenomenological seeing takes our full body experience into the experience of otherness and enables us to make a communicative turn away from the realities that negatively impact our communicative abilities between self and other and self and self. This communicative turn transcends our experiences from a constrained totality to an open infinite space of possibilities and potentialities.

As we seek understanding, the relationship between the presence of significance and absence of significance, is primary. Therefore, we seek understanding through transformative leisure because we come to a natural attitude that includes an "anticipation of consciousness-in-and-for-itself; its forgetfulness of itself is already the path by which it may come to self recognition."[12] Contemplation that enables one to return to the things themselves which come before our self knowledge or self behavior is a natural position. It becomes through this position that people transcend their physical body. We get to this natural attitude by way of tending to transformative leisure in our lives.

Our natural attitude emerges out of transformative leisure but it is the coupling with our corporeal experiences that lead us to transcendence beyond the flatly scripted world in which we find ourselves. When we experience our environments, we do this in a corporeal sense which means that the world is more like a labyrinth that contains in betweenness paths that go somewhere or nowhere. In this labyrinth we experience ourselves with others, sometimes in known and other times in unknown places. Our bodies experience the labyrinth where we connect, blend, and cross over others. We may not see where we are or where are might be because our experiences bend between ourselves and others. Together, our corporeal experiences in labyrinth and our natural attitudes combined transcend and propel us beyond

---

12 John O'Neill, *Perception, Expression, and History: The Social Phenomenology of Maurice Merleau-Ponty* (Evanston, IL: Northwestern University Press, 1970), 21.

the mystery and, while not always providing answers to our questions or mysteries, we are prepared to experience the serendipitous. Transformative leisure, in its purest sense, transcends the mundane and opens us up to new ideas and potentiality.

Alterity opens meaning when we begin by approaching an activity inwardly, within one's self, in full reflexion, before one is able to communicate outwardly with others. But we must consider that human begins are essentially social beings. We construct social realities so that we can live with others—by choice. Even if we want to be hermits or if we intentionally want to live outside of a social order, we still need to communicate with others, broadly defined, whether inanimate objects or objects of nature that live otherwise than human, we still need to be social beings. It is that need to be social, to live with others that becomes primordial to our existence. So, seeking transformative leisure through our understanding of our responsibility for the other enables us to start outside ourselves so that we can seek inside ourselves. Human freedom makes the idea of alterity challenging to us, especially in a world confronted by distractions and violence. Though we never can be released from this violence of the otherness and the other, we must start there in order to understand why we need to reflect inward. This condition is inescapable.

Understanding that a key aspect of ethicality in transformative leisure is alterity, a consideration of transformative leisure as a virtue ethic provides balance to this turning toward the other by turning toward the self in relation to the other through a reflexive virtue ethic. Josef Pieper's virtue ethics provides that balance in this chapter. Introducing the philosophy of Josef Pieper into this discussion is natural because of his commitment to leisure having philosophical ground and his moral stance on the importance of virtues in our lives. While Pieper's theological perspective is everpresent in his writings, it is not of central application to this work. Pieper's contribution wholly situates transformative leisure as an ethic by which one can live one's life. The ethicality found in alterity does not have the quality of samness as the ethicality in Josef Pieper's virtue ethic. However, both ethics involve doing and being, both ethics privilege ontological ethicality, and both ethics transcend the mundane of everyday experiences. Levinas's ethics as first philosophy and Pieper's virtue ethics provide a balance to the ethicality of transformative leisure as it transcends virtue and apriori aspects to all doing and being. By inviting the ethical philosophies of

Levinas and Pieper into this discussion, a balanced and unique virtue ethic is presented that permits transformative leisure to not only be life-giving but also life-sustaining.

TRANSFORMATIVE LEISURE: TRANSCENDENCE IN VIRTUE ETHICS

The concept of virtue ethics is different from principle-based or duty-based ethics in that a principle or duty implies a judgment about right and wrong actions or the notion of actions or principles that are either good or evil.[13] A basic virtue ethic emphasizes the individual and makes judgments about good and evil related to the person's traits and or their volition. Virtue ethics dominated the classical Greek world. In the *Nicomachean Ethics*, Aristotle was concerned about the end of all human action, which was deemed the highest good that a human being could achieve and this good would be attained through human action in the company of others, not isolated from them. The idea of what virtue means should not be confused with the question of what "ought" to be done. Virtue is a "beneficial disposition, habit, or trait which a person posses or aspires to posses."[14] Traditional ethics that emphasize principles of duty are only half of the picture. A virtue ethic would add an important perspective often less attended to in traditional ethical paradigms. Aristotle's moral views were grounded in particular character traits that provide a contrast between *doing* and *being*. Aristotle's basic question had to do with asking "what shall I be" instead of focusing on "what shall I do" and this focus represented a relationship between doing and being while privileging being over doing. For Aristotle, an ethic of being includes an ethic of Doing but the ethic of Being encompasses both Being and Doing. Just because one does something does not mean that person has particular moral qualities – sometimes people act for reasons other than a moral impulse. The notion of acting accordingly is situated in one's exteriority and avoids the interior (ethic of Being). An ethic of Doing and Being involves both interiority and exteriority, the privilege occurs in the interiority of one's virtue (Being).

---

13   Thomas Beauchamp, *Philosophical Ethics: An Introduction to Moral Philosophy* (New York: McGraw-Hill, 1982; Stephen Toulmin, *Reason in Ethics* (Cambridge, MA: Cambridge University Press, 1968).

14   Beauchamp, *Philosophical Ethics*, 150.

This chapter introduces transformative leisure as a virtue ethic and in doing so, situates the work of Josef Pieper as central to the project of explicating this particular virtue ethic. Transformative leisure, as a virtue ethic becomes an ethic of Being. I've selected Josef Pieper's virtue ethics to lay the groundwork for this part of our discussion because his virtue ethics are embodied through the transcendence of persons.

JOSEF PIEPER'S VIRTUE PHILOSOPHY

Josef Pieper wrote the most significant treatise on leisure in the twentieth century.[15] A medieval scholar and philosopher, much of Josef Pieper's work is concerned with virtues. His other work is lesser known in secular arenas but they are worth discussing to explicate virtue ethics in the spirit of Pieper's project. In this section, I look at selected works to foreshadow my consideration of transformative leisure as a virtue ethic. In his work, *The Four Cardinal Virtues* and *A Brief Reader on the Virtues of the Human Heart*, Pieper maps out a virtue philosophy of Being that can be tied into his philosophy of leisure related to the human condition.[16] Pieper's perspective reminds us about the nature of leisure and how leisure constitutes a good life, a virtuous life, the foundation of culture, and necessary nourishment for the human soul/interiority. While Pieper's body of philosophy is immense, his books are generally small in size but profound in content. As a general concern, the main aspects of his work center on the following concepts or conditions: human virtue, belief, knowledge, hope/despair, love, happiness, contemplation, joy, human authenticity, prudence, justice, courage, temperance, being-truth-good, reason, experience, freedom, and, of course, leisure. Though this is not an exhaustive list, it is representative of Pieper's philosophy.

Josef Pieper was born in 1904 in Germany. He attended the *Gymnasium Paulinum*, where he was exposed to the work of Thomas Aquinas. Pieper's discovery of Aquinas would come to have a profound influence on his scholarship, philosophy, and contribution to the academy. What becomes most important in this discussion is the

---

15   Josef Pieper, *Leisure: The Basis of Culture* (New York: Pantheon Books, 1952).

16   Josef Pieper, *A Brief Reader of the Virtues of the Human Heart* (San Francisco, CA: Ignatius Press, 1991); *The Four Cardinal Virtues*, (Notre Dame, IN: University of Notre Dame Press, 2007).

link between his virtue philosophy to transformative leisure in such a way that a virtue ethic emerges as an ethic of being in transcendence.

I chose to highlight some of Pieper's works that represent the main threads of his philosophy. In doing so, I make a stronger connection between transformative leisure and an ontological ethic of being. The four books are: *Leisure, the Basis of Culture; The Four Cardinal Virtues; In Defense of Philosophy;* and *Faith, Hope, Love.* At the end of these summaries, a map of his virtue philosophy will be drawn that illuminates leisure as a virtue ethic, an ethic of Being.

THE FIRST BOOK:
LEISURE, THE BASIS OF CULTURE

In his *Leisure, the Basis of Culture,* Josef Pieper suggested that leisure is a catalyst for catharsis of the human spirit as it releases one from the oppression of the self. Pieper began by establishing a definition of leisure etymologically and then moved forward through reason to provide a textured account of its classical origins.[17] Ultimately, leisure is situated theologically as it becomes inescapably linked to celebration, festival, and worship that removed one from everyday work-a-day toil in the world. Pieper reminded the modern world of the philosophical foundation of the act of leisure as a philosophical act itself.

The first part of *Leisure, the Basis of Culture* defines leisure philosophically and describes its action which begins with a contemplative spirit removed from everyday business and goal-seeking actions. Pieper reminded us that transformative leisure is actually hard work, not laziness or idleness. In fact, our actions in leisure have more at stake in the sense that this kind of contemplatively driven action is what cultivates one's soul and enables one to engage the Other in an authentic spirit. The second part of his first book describes the philosophical act itself. Pieper argued that the doing of leisure is a philosophical act that, if practiced daily, enables one to philosophize. In essence, doing leisure habituates one's ability to reason, to philosophize, or as Pieper stated, to wonder. Wonder is a way of playing with ideas that enables one to see beyond the obvious or beyond the emotional aspect. It is the act of wonder that permits the transformation that often emerges from the action of leisure. While this is perhaps an under abbreviated account of Pieper's *Leisure, the Basis of Culture,* it provides

---

17   Pieper, *Leisure.*

us with a starting place from which we understand how Pieper defined leisure and what he suggested are the significant outcomes from a life that engages leisure. The important aspect here is the idea that leisure cultivates one's ability to philosophize and see the world differently in order to Be in the world differently. In this case, leisure is ontologically significant and connected to the nurturing of one's Being and one's Being-in-the-world. Pieper's commitment to virtue is a primary force in this philosophy.

THE SECOND BOOK:
THE FOUR CARDINAL VIRTUES

In his *The Four Cardinal Virtues*, Pieper identified the four cardinal virtues as prudence, justice, fortitude, and temperance. In this very brief summary of his text, each virtue is defined, the idea of what Pieper means as "cardinal" is explored, and leisure is illuminated as being undeniably linked to the idea of virtue.[18] Prudence, as the first virtue listed by Pieper, is the mother of all of the other cardinal virtues, the *genitrix virtutum*. Pieper elaborated on this concept and, unlike the contemporary understanding of prudence as a timorous small-minded, self-preservational concern, he asserted that prudence is the realization that the good presupposes knowledge of reality, which means that our actions are appropriate to the real situation in which we find ourselves. This means that one does what is right and good, presupposing that one knows the reality, the real, of a given situation. To know this sense of real, one must be able to *see* the real and we see the real through philosophizing.

The contemporary understanding of prudence is weaker than its originative definition. Today, prudence is connoted by adjectives such as small-minded, self-preserved, perhaps selfishly concerned about one's self, or rigid in perspective and experience. Yet, these utilitarian connotations fall short of the actual meaning of prudence, which is that prudence is part of the classical definition of goodness; that prudence is a noble seeking toward the classical notion of what is good; and that virtue or virtuousness is prudent. This understanding of prudence is elevated to a higher plane and it is not together with worldly things, events, or conditions. The second cardinal virtue is justice, which implies justice is a habit (*habitus*), whereby one renders to each

---

18   Pieper, *The Four Cardinal Virtues*.

one or other what is due without deviation. It is a perpetual pursuit. Pieper derived his understanding of justice from Plato's account that stated it is the idea that each person is to receive what is due based upon her/his own actions. Pieper questioned whether this "due" is an inalienable possession but he ultimately suggested that justice cannot be fully developed outside of a complete moral doctrine, which means that justice cannot be considered or defined independently of other aspects of morality. In fact, justice only becomes intelligible when it is within the story of a human being, within a moral context and within lived action because justice is related to one's relation with the Other. Pieper suggested that justice pertains to the idea of righteousness in the sense that it is not limited to the doing of a right thing but also, and more importantly, "*to be* just as well." [19]

Finally, Pieper privileged three forms of justice, which have to do with 1) reciprocal justice – or relations of individuals to one another; 2) ministering justice – or relations of the social whole to individuals, and; 3) legal or general justice – pertaining to the relations of the individual to the social whole.[20] Pieper covered areas involving restitution and distributive justice, and the limits of justice, each of which are situated with an ethical concern for moving toward what is the good. Justice is an ethically-laden way of being as we live among and with Others. In order to attain Pieper's justice, one must be able to reason and wonder about ideas in order to seek out toward that particular good.

Fortitude is the third cardinal virtue, which presupposes a vulnerability toward death – Pieper stated that "all fortitude stands in the presence of death" and it implies a readiness to die, to fall, in battle.[21] In this stance of readiness, one takes risks and this highest level of fortitude is martyrdom. This does not mean that one is fearless. In fact, fear is part of the endurance and attack of fortitude. But it means to stand up for the good that one knows is right. Fortitude enables one to move, in fear, toward the good that one seeks. Along with this idea of fortitude is the notion of suffering, which means to endure in times of difficulty. So, in fortitude, one doesn't not give up, instead, one continues to press forward toward the good in sight. It would be unethical to give up the battle rather; one must be willing to lose in order to gain.

19   Pieper, *The Four Cardinal Virtues*, 63.
20   Ibid, 71.
21   Ibid, 117.

Finally, the last cardinal virtue, is temperance. This virtue is related to the first three virtues while being distinguished from them because it refers exclusively to the active person. Temperance aims at the person her or himself instead of the action of giving up for others or doing something for others. Temperance suggests that a person should look inward at her or himself and it points toward a realization of an order in oneself. Today, temperance is thought of as a moderation of vices but this severely limits our understanding and Pieper's point. The *telos* of temperance requires a person to search her/his inner self and put one's self in order – only then can an inner serenity occur. Temperance enables cultivation of one's inner space because that is its only focus; the playground of temperance is one's interiority.

While these brief explanations of Pieper's work on the four virtues are barely sufficient to fully play with Pieper's entire philosophy, they do represent a broad range of ideas that move us toward an ethic of Being emerging from transformative leisure. The notion of "cardinal" though is reflective of his marriage of philosophy and theology. These are "cardinal" virtues because these virtues lead one to the divine. The path to the divine, for Pieper, is to become what God intended one to become. Pieper would argue that the human being ought to become what he *is to be* and therefore not what he (merely) already is. Attaining these cardinal virtues is accessed through the action of transformative leisure. Transformative leisure sets forth to attain the authentic experience of these virtues. Fruits of these four cardinal virtues lead to the next two texts to be summarized because without the cultivation of these virtues, one's life becomes empty and perhaps a shadow of the person meant to be.

THE THIRD BOOK: *IN DEFENSE OF PHILOSOPHY*

Pieper's *In Defense of Philosophy* is a small but significant work because he philosophizes through classical form, using logos to get at the idea of philosophy itself – to not err in philosophizing but to at first defeat it though criticism and then to restore or resurrect philosophy though reason itself, the same thing that attempted to defeat it. Pieper considered the objection to whether or not the philosophical question can be answered at all and the value of philosophy as it seemingly has no utility. He suggested that philosophy is no ordinary activity and that is it essentially connected to praxis. He argued that sophists were dangerous because they distorted philosophical structures in the interest of their own gain and opinions, rather than looking for the good.[22] Other criticisms of philosophy include the idea of the tensions between science and philosophy and the lack of precise language in science's critique of philosophy, as well as approaching philosophy without or outside of presuppositions.

Faith, revelation, tradition, and theology are starting places for philosophy and academic sophistry has no place in these starting places or in philosophizing. Pieper stated that philosophy is absolute questioning and absolute freedom that requires a respect between philosophy and science and defends the ideal of living out this openness of the human mind. In short, *In Defense of Philosophy* addresses the tensions between philosophy and science by addressing the criticisms imposed by science upon philosophy. Pieper uses scholastic disputation, a medieval form of argumentation, designed to attend thoroughly to the opponent in an open and constructive manner. Pieper demonstrated that argumentation is the best, most effective way to engage in fortitude (standing up for philosophy in the face of philosophy's execution), justice (delivery of what is due to sophistry in the academy), temperance (becoming what he ought to become, a defender of philosophy), and lastly but most importantly, prudence, the noble task of seeking, seeing, and pursuing the good, all of which science cannot attain. The philosophy that Pieper defends against science is a philosophy imbued with leisure. Finally, the last text considered deals with three basic virtues that intertwine with the four cardinal virtues and that are undeniably related to transformative leisure as well.

THE FOURTH BOOK: *FAITH, HOPE, LOVE*

The publication of *Faith, Hope, Love* came about as a result of combining three previously published separate treatises, (*Über den Glauben*), *Belief and Faith: A Philosophical Tract* (1962/1963); (*Über die Hoffnung*), *On Hope* (1935/1977); and (*Über die Liebe*), *On Love* (1972/1992).[23] Written at different times in Pieper's life, and within changing historical moments, Pieper provided a discussion with intersecting points related to the virtues of faith, hope, and love for everyday communicative actions. In his discussion of faith, Pieper began with

22 Josef Pieper, *In Defense of Philosophy* (San Francisco, CA: Ignatius Press, 1992).

23 Josef Pieper, *Faith, Hope, Love* (San Francisco, CA: Ignatius Press, 1997)

the fundamental types of attitudes, being: doubt; opinion; knowledge; and belief. Belief, for Pieper meant to consider something as being true based upon testimony of another. Belief cannot be forced upon another or demanded upon another, rather one believes only if one wants to believe. Belief assumes revelation but in the modern world there was an absence of or silence from God, rendering belief implicit and sometimes, nonexistent. Pieper asked the question, is it good to believe? His response suggested that belief wasn't just a human virtue, but that belief is a participation in the knowledge of God and in divine reality (and reality of the divine). So, doubt is essential because that is what initiates one's reason and philosophizing toward an opinion that is cultivated from gaining knowledge, which ultimately shapes one's beliefs. Faith is an ongoing philosophical action that ultimately comes from the philosophical act Pieper described in his treatise on *Leisure*.

The basic virtue of hope is closely related to the cardinal virtue of fortitude. Hope is the virtue of the not yet in that it is existence in the state of being that is *on its way* to fulfillment, an orientation toward something; it is a *telos* yet undefined or perhaps, unknown. Pieper situates hope as a theological virtue as Jesus Christ is the foundation of that sacred hope. Along with hope comes despair, a character of existence, both of which can remain hidden in an anticipation of non-fulfillment. Fear is also a counterpart to hope, but in fear comes trust, as Pieper suggested, quoting from Psalms 115:11, "They who fear the Lord trust in the Lord". Pieper's treatise on hope points one toward the *telos* of hope, God. The next virtue, love, is complex. Pieper admitted to struggling with his attention to love, so much so that he did not write about love until late in his scholarly and philosophical development.

Love is not a thing. In all forms of love there is one common thread: approval. Love is confirming through the knowing that one is loved by another which cultivates a primal trust and knowing that one pleases another (whether secular or sacred, love is a confirmation of one's Being). In Pieper's doctrine of love there are aspects that include this notion of approval along with some others such as: eros or erotic love; friendships of love; maternal and paternal love; and selfless self-love. Each of these can destroy or create but the power of love resides within its perfection, a perfection that transforms the individual and the relationship, and perhaps brings them closer to the divine.

These four books are representative of Pieper's larger body of philosophical treatises. While the summaries presented here merely touch
on a portion of the ideas in each work, we begin to see the threads
weaving together, pointing toward his understanding of virtue ethics.
Pieper should be recognized as a standard bearer of virtue ethics especially from a theological perspective. However, while often leading
to God, a virtue ethic can also be found valuable in a secular sense,
leading to the *supra*, the highest good that a human being can achieve,
whatever tradition from which one negotiates life. This is not moral
relativism, rather, what it means is that in a postmodern world there is
a mutual and reciprocal respect for beliefs and traditions across a wide
array of paradigms, though they compete, they are mutually respectable. The highest good, for Pieper, was a human being's potential to get
to God. The highest good in a general sense is the attainment of one's
fullest potential, whether that is a path to God, Allah, Buddha, Zeus,
or Mab, it doesn't matter, it is the attainment of one's fullest potential—that is key to achieve the good. In mapping out a framework for
virtue ethics furthers my point that transformative leisure in action is
a phenomenological experience of a lived virtue ethic.

TRANSFORMATIVE LEISURE AND
ETHICAL TRANSCENDENCE

Perhaps beginning with Pieper's four cardinal virtues is appropriate to
start the journey toward identifying transformative leisure as a virtue
ethic. Prudence, the mother of all virtues reminds us of nobility, the
noble path of finding one's fullest potential. It is a path unknown to us
but we are responsible for forging it with justice, fortitude, and temperance. Understanding the thick descriptions of these virtues is one
thing but to actually 'do' them or 'live' them in action or more precisely,
experience them is quite another accomplishment. The habituation of
a life imbued with transformative leisure shapes these virtues in our
daily actions and Being. Consider that transformative leisure begins
in a contemplative spirit, a hermeneutic humility that permits one to
philosophize, to engage authentically the philosophical act posited by
Pieper in *Leisure: The Basis of Culture*. This is a prudent discovery,
experience, encounter, and way of approaching one's life. Once hermeneutic humility is cultivated, one can embrace this humility in the
quest toward justice by understanding more than adequately what

is due from one's own or another's actions. As hermeneutic humility is cultivated, one can better understand fortitude in that along with endurance there comes suffering. This adheres to the later argument that transformative leisure is hard work or is at least, not easy to do. Engagement of transformative leisure requires an authentic abstention of some things, an absence from the world in a way that may be uncomfortable but that can only cultivate one's notion of temperance, which is constitutive of one's Being, rather than one's doing. This is the heart of where transformative leisure becomes a virtue ethic, an ethical way of doing that shapes one's communicative Being, which is the essential nature of a virtue ethic as opposed to a deontological ethic or other ethical paradigms. This is an opening for the discussion of transformative leisure as a virtue ethic wholly situated within a communicative context. Even though virtue ethics has to do with one's Being more so than one's doing, Being and doing are inescapably linked. Therefore, we cannot talk about a virtue ethic outside of a communication ethic because our Being and doing always-already imposes upon Others.

This chapter clearly advances the idea that transformative leisure, as a virtue ethic wholly situated within an invitational communicative framework, cultivates the action of Being in the world. A good is the value center of a particular communication ethic.[24] The good is what is most important and what is held in highest regard. The good is the supposed responsibility toward the other that can only fully emerge from a hermeneutic of humility. It is in this hermeneutic humility that our selfless self-love can emerge while limiting a very human desire to be driven by or act from agency. A key aspect of transformative leisure as a virtue ethic is concerned with shaping one's Being through hermeneutic humility and can be briefly teased out through the idea of alterity that foreshadows a subsequent chapter.

The ethical relation between human beings is the foundation of all knowledge.[25] The idea of ethics as first philosophy implies that ethics are the ground upon which we engage otherness and it is central to meeting the Other. The notion of first philosophy comes from Aristotle's *Metaphysics* in which he inquires about the study of being,

---

24 Ronald C. Arnett, J. H. Fritz, L. M. Bell, Communication Ethics Literacy: Dialogue and Difference (New Thousand Oaks, CA: Sage, 2008).
25 Aristotle, "Metaphysics," in *The Basic Works of Aristotle*, ed. Richard McKeon (New York: Modern Library, 2001a), 689-934.

what it means to be. In general, the study of metaphysics is undeniably related and intertwined with first philosophy. Levinas's argument for ethics as first philosophy encapsulates transformative leisure as a virtue ethic since it is in the realm in the doing of transformative leisure that we ensure our ability to begin with the other and negate self will and agency as we concern ourselves with the nature of our Being. Yet it is not through the doing that transformative leisure exemplifies a virtue ethic, it is through the doing of transformative leisure that Being becomes transformed. The action of transformative leisure is really, perhaps, secretly, working toward a transformation on its own, manifesting as a by-product of a synthesis of actions experienced within a hermeneutic humility that embraces the Other implicitly in one's interiority. In other words, leisure begins in one's interiority. Transformative leisure as a virtue ethic embodies a concern for Being qua Being that cannot be found in the worldly action of doing. In this relation, Being and doing remain counterparts.

For example, it is easy to get caught up in a world of work. It is only through leisure that one can nurture one's own communicative Being. So, in my life, when I get caught up in unceasing mundane tasks of everyday toil, I can become overwhelmed in the interiority of my communicative Being, yet I continue to move through my daily tasks as if I am unresponsive to the violence of this unrelenting toil. I need to play my violin. I've studied my violin since 1969 and it has not been easy, in fact there have been times where learning a passage or a new scale or a new string quartet, that I am left exhausted, yet it is that exhaustion that nurtures my interiority. Without this kind of habituated transformative leisure in my life I am engulfed in tacit violence of a life without inner cultivation. The tacit violence to which I referred is toward myself and all other communicative relationships in which I am embedded. Transformative leisure provides me a recuperative outlet that cultivates my interior character and eventually this manifests in the enrichment of my communicative Being enabling me to take that communicative turn toward the Other in an ethical way.

The condition of interestedness or agency is embedded within a nonreflective consciousness, a consciousness without a pre-reflective condition, but by embracing our responsibility toward the Other we can remedy this condition by moving toward a condition of disinterestedness that transcends conditions of totality. Leisure as a virtue ethic is disinterested and embedded within a hermeneutic humility that is driven by prudence, open to justice, and apprehending fortitude in order to cultivate temperance. Josef Pieper argued that, "[i]n the virtue of prudence the ring of the active life is rounded out and closed, is completed and perfected; for man, drawing on his experience of reality, acts in and upon reality, thus realizing himself in decision and in act" which points to what this essay contends is the heart of a virtue ethic, it is a realization of or emphasis upon one's Being more so than one actions.[26] Acknowledging transformative leisure as a virtue ethic is paramount to the understanding that it emerges through a hermeneutic humility which is phenomenologically and ontologically situated within an experience that shapes one's Being.

CONCLUSION

Transformative leisure in the context of discourse, self, and community point us toward a transcendence beyond the known and puts us on a path toward recuperative relief from struggling to exist in an already difficult world. Within our phenomenological experiences we negotiate between "passive and active moments of possibility" [27] and it is the playful excitement of these moments that reveal the nature of transformative leisure to us. In transformative leisure everyone begins where we find ourselves and we experience freedom of play that negotiates, intervenes, and expresses ideas to us. We exist within a constant state of potential *poiesis* but the world around us diverts our attention and often deceives us. As we lose the ability to transcend these diversions, we risk becoming alienated from our potential; we risk losing our natural attitude.

In this unnatural condition, the possibilities of the *not-yet* are quelled and this cripples our existence without our awareness or knowing. This is where we lose ourselves; we lose our capacity to do or to know; we become a shadow if ourselves and what we-might-have-been. To save ourselves and to transcend this potential of nonexistence, we turn to transformative leisure. Our bodies play a role in the possibility of self disclosing to others, and we do this through our corporeal habits.[28] In a life practiced with transformative leisure, the body recedes from

26 Pieper, *The Four Cardinal Virtues*, 55.

27 Ramsey Eric Ramsey, *The Long Path to Nearness: A Contribution to a Corporeal Philosophy of Communication and the Groundwork for an Ethics of Relief* (New York: Humanity Books, 1998), 9.

28 Ramsey, *The Long Path to Nearness*.

conscious awareness because *being in play* is both present in action
and absent in mind as a receding action. The mindful habit of transformative leisure is a conscious embodiment; a reflective action with
an absence of intent and a presence of tending to something within a
situation of possibilities.

Transformative leisure, as a philosophy of the mind, holds promise
toward an Epicurean transcendence. Much like Epicurus (341BCE-
270 BCE) who advocated that contemplation was a pleasure of the
soul and who warned against the destructive nature of competition, we
must be mindful in our contemporary environment of technological
propagation and global awareness. In the *Vatican Sentences*, Epicurus
admitted that a life is wasted if it is a life without leisure and we can be
certain he meant transformative leisure, not recreation, though he did
see contemplation slightly different from Aristotle because of the emphasis and value he placed on pleasure; for Epicurus, contemplation is
pleasurable.[29] In his *Letter to Menoeceus* Epicurus also indicated that
we cannot be too old to be mindful about the health of our soul—
it is never too late. Unlike some popular judgments about Epicurean
philosophy as being driven by hedonism, Epicurus sought wisdom
through pleasure though not a bodily pleasure, but pleasure for the
sake of itself in acts involving contemplation, modesty, and moderation. This kind of action takes practice and discipline. Epicurean insight takes us back to the humble Garden of contemplation, modesty,
and moderation to a life that passes over many sensual pleasures in
pursuit of the good life that embodies pleasure, a life without bodily
pain, and a life with a peaceful soul. Therefore in an Epicurean spirit,
transformative leisure provides an enriching potential to our human
condition.

As we think of embodied consciousness, it is "the occasion whence
we enact communicative praxis …[that] demands philosophical consideration."[30] In transformative leisure there is a *whereness* that negotiates between our finite bodies and the infinite possibilities of our
experiences. Transcendence beyond the curious is an awareness that
we experience through wonder. Now, let's put this together; transformative leisure in discourse, action, community, and transcendence to
consider how we might *tend* to leisure.

29 E. Brown, "Contemplative Withdrawal in the Hellenistic Age,"
    Philosophical Studies 137, (2008): 79-89.
30 Ramsey, *The Long Path to Nearness*, 62.

CHAPTER 5

CONCLUSION

TENDING TO TRANSFORMATIVE LEISURE

Humility attempts to ensure a guarding against the transgression of arrogance, when arrogance is seen as the false belief that one has achieved complete or total a-whereness

–Ramsey Eric Ramsey

Wonder always awaits us

–Les Amis

Exploring transformative leisure through Calvin Schrag's framework of discourse, action, community, and transcendence situates the *tending* to leisure after postmodernity in a helpful light. By following this path, we have become attuned to transformative leisure in discourse as we have listened to the *who*, the authors that cared about leisure in the past up through the present; by becoming attuned to transformative leisure in action, we have considered the *how* and *what* by observing the communicative actions of those engaging in leisure—observing *what* kind of action is engaged and *how* it is phenomenologically different from other kinds of action; by becoming attuned to transformative leisure in community we gained a sense of *who* is responding to others, *how* they are responding, and *why* they choose a particular response in a given socioeconomic and political environment; and finally, by becoming attuned to transformative leisure in transcendence, we learned to see openings that invite possibilities and potentialities that cultivate our humanness by texturing the interior condition of the mind per-mitting us entrance into a realm beyond physical limits and closings.

Life is a gift. We are obligated to live a life worth living and in doing so, to seek out the other, the collective, and the *what might come to be*. As human agents, we cannot do this without thought or practice. Like doing yoga, our bodies perform better after stretching beyond with balance and corporeal poise in a practiced fashion. We cannot become a yogi if we do not engage yoga as a habit and a life style. It takes time, practice, and presence for yoga to affect our minds and bodies. Likewise, transformative leisure requires the same kind of commitment and if we practice it in our lives, we will be happier with ourselves and better able to have healthy and sustainable relationships with others. This book has explored a variety of environments, philos-ophies, and conditions that inform us how transformative leisure is a type of spiritual exercise that can foster cultivation of our humanness by connecting us, as human beings, artfully with others.

Linda Wiener and Ramsey Eric Ramsey remind us that our world in which we live is not perfect as, "[i]t requires neither research scien-tists nor philosophers to persuade us that much is wrong and much is missing in the world today."[1] Questions of ethical, political, social, en-vironmental, and interpersonal disruption confront us daily. Whether the issue at hand involves questions of war, genocide, global warming, environmental disasters, or the technological/scientific revolution, it becomes clear that the human race encounters daily challenges in con-fronting these disruptions. Ethical paradigms compete and issues of power and control fuel much of the discourse while communicative actions are often questioned. The world has become expediently divi-sive and it is not always easy to figure out how we ought to begin or to situate our communicative engagements. Starting from a philosoph-ical mindset can give us a nudge in a helpful direction. This starting place offers ontological insight that permits us to experience hope—hope that the human race can meet in a communicative space where transversal discourse can begin to tend to these disruptions in a fair, just, and equitable way. Finding that space begins with the individual and the individual must begin in wonder and contemplation.

Wonder calls out to us *and* it calls us out. Wonder invites us to move—it solicits our action. This call, however, is not external. Rather,

1   Linda Wiener, R. E. Ramsey, *Leaving Us to Wonder: An Essay On the Questions Science Can't Ask* (New York: SUNY, 2005).

wonder confronts us from within and puts us in motion.[2] Wonder invites the cultivation of aesthetic sensibilities and hermeneutic humility that, when tended together, overwhelm our being. It is only through our engagement of wonder that there is anything out there that which permits a being *thereness*.

Wonder is an ontological, phenomenological, and existential condition that reveals infinite potentiality in being. This condition goes beyond a scientific curiosity or imagination that points us toward something—this pointing toward something is a kind of calculation which does not provide an opportunity for an exercise of free and thoughtful deliberation.[3] Wonder invites existence that is seemingly inescapable and serendipitous. Wonder permits a new temporal order to emerge which is ontological and outside of any chronological directive. This kind of meeting through wonder points us toward the future and gives us hope while opening our eyes to our being-in-the-world. Without wonder we are unfit for the participation in public discourse; without wonder we lack the capacity to be a good citizen, a responsible citizen, and an active participant in the lifeworld around us.

Wonder permits a disinterestedness that becomes a *habitus*. In making transformative leisure a *habitus*, a way of life, we can look toward Plato and Hadot's spiritual exercises. Spiritual exercises are paths we choose to take us somewhere in a disinterestedness—guiding and preparing us for the journey. This path is hard work and must be part of one's daily life—it is a life style choice. This path is also a critical path undergirded by philosophical insight and a hope for learning.[4] The permission of wonder in our lives is the key to unlocking the future for communicative beings.

But what does wonder have to do with transformative leisure? Wiener and Ramsey argue that "experience is a living category that escapes all attempts of scientific reduction and can never be completely captured by its system of fact production."[5] The experience of transformative leisure is also a living category and also cannot be measured by any kind of science or fact. Wonder and transformative leisure

---

2 Les Amis, *Commemorating Epimetheus*, trans. S. Pluháček (West Lafayette, IN: Purdue University Press, 2009).

3 Wiener and Ramsey, *Leaving*.

4 Ramsey Eric Ramsey, "Somehow Learning to Live: On Being Critical," *Communication and Critical/Cultural Studies* 8, no. 1 (2001a): 88-92.

5 Wiener and Ramsey, *Leaving*, 121.

are both metaphysical and transcendent in that they can neither be formally choreographed nor empirically measured because they occur both in inside and outside—in one's interiority and one's exteriority. Wonder begins as the interior action of the first moments of transformative leisure, contemplation.

Cultivation of the imagination through wonder begins in contemplation. Through contemplation we engage an aesthetic play which is, "free association of ideas...making an attempt of creating a free form...mixed with the acts of a blind instinct." [6] In contemplation we become. We become free to experience aesthetic sensibilities that create meaning in something. In contemplation we are not hindered or tied to any particular thing, rather we are seeking something that which is not known. The troubling aspect of transformative leisure for many people is its situatedness within infinity. The idea that we cannot know where it takes us or what kind of transformative action might occur to our being is frightening to many who want some kind of foreknowledge related to their actions. This desire to always know or predict with certainty is an aspect of totality in which one can never grow toward their individual or collective potential.

Marcus Aurelius wrote his Mediations between 178-180 CE. In these writings he captured the spirit of transformative leisure when he stated that one ought to acquire the "contemplative way of seeing . . . constantly attend to it, and exercise yourself."[7] Aurelius meant that the exercise of seeing contemplatively is truly a philosophical act in which one tends to one's thoughts in a free and infinite movement of play. He urged his readers to hasten to examine their interior faculty that rules judgment and actions. He urged this because of the very nature of the social system in which every human being is a part. In this argument, Aurelius connected the interior and the exterior, two seemingly oppositional forces. He revealed that the exterior is dependent upon the interior. He suggested that one ought to acquire the contemplative way of life much like Pierre Hadot asserts that philosophy is a way of life. Contemplative action is unceasing. In contemplation, one sees the rational soul, one can see it, analyze it, and change it or permit it to be changed. Aurelius argued that there is no other way to do philosophy

6   Friedrich Schiller, *Letters Upon the Aesthetic Education of Man* (Whitefish, MT: Kessinger Publishing, 2004), 68.

7   Marcus Aurelius, Meditations (Roslyn, NY: Walter J. Black Publications, 1945), 107.

other than through a contemplative approach that gives us permission to wonder. It is the action of transformative leisure that is the philosophical act and it should be one's way of life.

Pierre Hadot's affirmation, philosophy as a way of life, reminds us that aesthetic perception of the world can be a model for a philosophical perception of the world. Transformation of one's worldview is intimately and inescapably tied to particular kinds of exercises which involve the mind's concentration upon some thing or things. This description is more specifically Hadot's understanding of wonder. The significance of this kind of exercise as occurring within "the instant"[8] becomes central to the action and outcome of a given experience. Wonder is an attitude that occurs within an instant that is a present moment in the entire universe or more aptly put, a moment that is situated within the infinite.

Hadot illuminates what he called spiritual exercises which are moments attending to the instant. It is through spiritual exercises that we learn to live. Through these exercises we seek out the good life and learn to live well. Spiritual exercises are habits—they should be habituated into our daily lives. Spiritual exercises enable us to temper our passions and obsessions so that we may able to see that which we seek. Spiritual exercises occur within a contemplative environment whereby we have a conversation with ourselves and sometimes with others and this communicative exchange has the potential to turn our lives upside down or inside out. Spiritual exercises can transform a life. This kind of interaction is free from inauthentic conditions—it is a process that causes one to be more fully aware of the world around the self and the landscape of the inner self; it is at once interior and exterior.

A life that practices transformative leisure is a life that engages spiritual exercises that we trust to guide us in our seeking and guard us from those passions and obsessions that might divert our movement or obscure our path toward the good life. Transformative leisure is a spiritual exercise because it involves inner contemplation and outer conversation. Transformative leisure has the potential to cause us to be wholly in our being which we often are not if we do not tend to philosophical acts that cultivate our interiority. In our saturated world of digital media, fast evolving social media, and ever-changing forms of mediated communication, we lose the ability to be wholly in

---

8   Pierre Hadot, *Philosophy as a Way of Life* (Malden, MA: Blackwell Publishing, 2009), 259.

our being because mediation is just that—something that is between something else. Media functions for a purpose and has great potential to make living in a global community easier and more effective than without it. At the same time, a wholly mediated environment obscures our humanity in such a way that we lose ourselves and our ability to be wholly present in our being. If we are wholly present in our being we are better able to be wholly present toward others. Transformative leisure permits, encourages, and shapes our ethicality toward the other because it ensures we are ethically present in and to ourselves. We begin with ourselves in wonder and we end up somewhere with someone else in some fashion.

Transformative leisure provides a reversal of the mundane—making possible a metamorphosis, a transformation of the self, a transformation of the other, or a transformation of the world. Both transformative leisure and the idea of a spiritual exercise involves investigation, reading of text (written/spoken/imaged), listening, attention/attending, self-mastery, and indifference to indifferent things—all of which are essential for the existence and application of a spiritual exercise. In transformative leisure, one gives attention to the present moment—the instant. A life without spiritual exercises invites us to worry about things that are needless or point us toward outcomes that we can never fully satisfy. Likewise, a life without transformative leisure is a life imbued with the unknown. It is through the *interiority* of the spiritual exercise that transformative leisure permits one to see *out there* and reach her or his human potential which cannot be known until it is achieved. There is hope and faith in the actions of transformative leisure, an activity we do for the sake of the activity itself but an action that heralds more power over our potentiality than we can really understand.

The action of transformative leisure prepares us to be competent communicators in the transversal space of communicative praxis. Since human beings are social beings by nature, we naturally want to live among others, so we must understand the most effective and ethical ways of this kind of social/political engagement. Calvin Schrag and Ramsey Eric Ramsey argued that transversal comprehension has the ability to manage conflicting interpretations between human beings which can keep communication open and productive because this experience occurs within a hermeneutical meeting space.[9]

9   Schrag and Ramsey, "Method and Phenomenological Research."

Transformative leisure habituates our communicative practices so that we are effective in that hermeneutical meeting place. The infinite possibilities that emerge from engaging in transformative leisure requires a humility that which permits and invites openness—freedom in openness. As we meet others in this hermeneutical meeting place we must not be afraid to permit a co-creation of meaning through you and your neighbor because we exist within a system comprised on ourselves and our neighbors that creates and shapes our social life with others. We dwell in the world with others but we have to live with ourselves. We must privilege our sociality if we want to seek the good life. We enhance our sociality through the contemplative experience of transformative leisure.

Transformative leisure should be considered a way of life – not a short recreative game or restful break from an over stimulated mediated world. Transformative leisure creates transcendence through the weaving together elements of wonder and slow in our everyday life. The marriage of interiority/exteriority and inside/outside privileges the poetic and permits a *poiesis* that cultivates the interiority/inside and exteriority/outside so we remain on the path toward the good life. It is through the experience of transformative leisure that we can embrace these spiritual exercises pointing us toward the good life and inviting us into the ongoing experience of learning who we are ourselves and who we are with other communicative beings at the present and into the future.

POSTSCRIPT

As I finish writing this book, I am also learning about Scottish fiddling with Jann Sparks, a friend and colleague in music. When we first met a few years ago we played together in a small orchestra gig. We had music to share but knew very little about each other. We exchanged phatic conversation at first but by the time of the performance (after just a couple of rehearsals) we began to talk more about music, performance, preferences, and past performance experiences. I also learned Jann's husband was a colleague of mine, Richard Sparks, who also teaches at Plymouth State University in the Business Department (at the time, now the College of Business Administration). Jann and I both love music and both experience music as leisure in our lives. Because we each have cultivated leisure in our lives, we had much to share and talk about. Our conversations have continued and we also still play together—as I mentioned above, we are playing Scottish fiddling/folk tunes. This is quite different for me as a classically trained violinist. When I am not playing with Jann, I am practicing my scales and reading (sight reading) new fiddling tunes so that I become intimately acquainted with different kinds of bowings, articulations, and rhythms inherent in Scottish fiddling. When we play together I am prepared though not perfect. Practicing is hard work. Playing and blending our sound in duets is hard work. Learning to follow Jann when she plays first violin takes focus and attention. I am sure she has the same concerns when I play first violin too. Together we play music and talk about the history of Scottish fiddling; we talk about how it is different from classical violin playing. We experiment with bowings, fingerings, dynamics, and articulations. Sometimes we agree; sometimes we don't. What we do not do is even more enlightening. We do not gossip; we do not insult each other; we do not get jealous of one another. We do share friendship; we do support each other even in disagreement; we find constructive and sustainable ways of being in the world together—we share in transformative leisure. My individual practicing and preparation for our playing is my leisure; our playing togetherness is also my leisure—both are hard work yet both experiences cultivate my interiority in ways that no other activity (that is not leisure) can do. If I lose everything else I have materially, I still have leisure because I can still play my violin and I can still think about musicality at a deep level. This is what transformative leisure does for us. It liberates us from descending into negative forms of communication or actions. Transformative leisure is healthy and sustains life toward a transcendence that we cannot force or forge intentionally. We slowly walk our path in wonder; we do this individually or with another—where we end up is unknown but it surprises us and we learn about our self and about others in the experience. Transformative leisure liberates us—let yourself experience this kind of liberation; potentiality awaits.

FINAL THOUGHTS

(FOR THOSE WHO STILL HAVE QUESTIONS)

Transformative leisure is not only for those who have money or for those who do not need to work for a living.

Transformative leisure is for human beings who want to attend to-the-things-themselves. So all of that money or all of that non-work associated time is meaningless unless an individual finds value in being with her or himself—and habituates in wonder.

Contemplation, reflection, self-reflexion, and engaging in play is all that is needed for one to embrace and do transformative leisure...the only privilege that occurs is in the privileging of ideas and the experience...

BIBLIOGRAPHY

FOR OPENING CHAPTER QUOTES

Amis, Les. *Commemorating Epimetheus.* Translated by S. Pluháček. West Lafayette, IN: Purdue University Press, 2009. 44

Arendt, Hannah. *The Human Condition.* 1958. Chicago, IL: University of Chicago Press, 1998. 131

Hadot, Pierre. *Philosophy as a Way of Life.* 1987. Translated by M. Chase. Malden, MA: Blackwell Publishing, 2009. 87

Levinas, Emmanuel. *The Levinas Reader.* Ed. Seán Hand. Malden, MA: Blackwell Publishers, 2000. 76

Marx, Karl. *Capital: A Critique of Political Economy.* 1894. Vol. 3. New York: Penguin Classics, 1993. 959

Merleau-Ponty, Maurice. *The Structure of Behavior.* 1942. Boston: Beacon Press, 1963. 223

O'Neill, J. *Perception, Expression, and History: The Social Phenomenology of Maurice Merleau-Ponty.* Evanston, IL: Northwestern University Press, 1970. 20

Pieper, Josef. *Leisure: The Basis of Culture.* 1952. South Bend, IN: St. Augustine Press, 1998. 31

Ramsey, Ramsey Eric. *The Long Path to Nearness: A Contribution to a Corporeal Philosophy of Communication and the Groundwork for an Ethics of Relief.* New York: Humanity Books, 1998. 78

———. "On the Dire Necessity of the Useless: Philosophical and Rhetorical Thoughts on Hermeneutics and Education in the Humanities." In *Education, Dialogue, and Hermeneutics.* Edited by P. Fairfield. New York: Continuum, 2011. 94

——— and David J. Miller. eds. *Experiences Between Philosophy and Communication: Engaging the Philosophical Contributions of Calvin O. Schrag.* New York: SUNY Press, 2003. 12

Schrag, C. O. *The Self After Postmodernity.* New Haven, CT: Yale University Press, 1997. 82

————."The Communicative Turn in the Dynamics of Philosophical Discourse." Keynote Speech delivered on June 3, 2010 at the National Communication ethics Conference, held at Duquesne University, 2010.

Wilde, Oscar. *The Soul of Man Under Socialism and Selected Critical Prose.* Edited by L. Dowling. New York: Penguin Classics, 1997. 10

BIBLIOGRAPHY

Adorno, Theodor. "Free time." 1969. *The culture industry: Selected essays on mass culture*, edited by J. Bernstein, London: Routledge, 1991.

Amis, Les. *Commemorating Epimetheus.* Translated by S. Pluháček. West Lafayette, IN: Purdue University Press, 2009.

Arendt, Hannah. *Eichmann in Jerusalem: A report on the banality of evil.* New York: Penguin Books, 1963.

———. *The human condition.* 1958. Chicago, IL: University of Chicago Press, 1998.

———. *The Jewish writings.* New York: Schocken Books, 2007.

———. *Rachel Varnhagen: The life of a Jewess.* Edited by L. Weissberg. Translated by R. Winston, C. Winston. Baltimore, MD: Johns Hopkins University Press, 1997.

Aristotle. *Nicomachean Ethics.* Oxford: Oxford University Press, 1998.

———. "Metaphysics." *The Basic Works of Aristotle*, edited by Richard McKeon, 689-934. New York: Modern Library, 2001.

———. "Politics." *The Basic Works of Aristotle*, edited by Richard McKeon, 1127-1324. New York: Modern Library, 2001.

Arneson, Pat. *Perspectives on Philosophy of Communication.* West Lafayette, IN: Purdue University Press, 2007.

Arnett, Ronald C. "Leisure and the Communicative Praxis of Craft." *Listening: Journal of Communication Ethics, Religion, and Culture* 46, no. 1 (2011): 21-36.

———. "The Responsive 'I': Levinas's Derivative Argument." *Argumentation & Advocacy* 40, no. 1 (2003): 39-50.

Arnett, Ronald C., Janie Harden Fritz, and Leeanne M. Bell. *Communication Ethics Literacy: Dialogue and Difference.* New York: Peter Lang, 2009.

Arnett, Ronald C., Pat Arneson, and Annette M. Holba. "Bridges Not Walls: The Communicative Enactment of Dialogic Storytelling." *Review of Communication*, 8, no. 3 (2008): 217- 234.

Audi, Robert, ed. *The Cambridge Dictionary of Philosophy.* New York: Cambridge University Press, 1999.

Aurelius, Marcus. *Meditations*. Roslyn, NY: Walter J. Black Publications, 1945.

Beauchamp, Thomas. *Philosophical Ethics: An Introduction to Moral Philosophy*. New York: McGraw-Hill, 1982.

Benhabib, Seyla. *The Reluctant Modernism of Hannah Arendt*. Walnut Creek, CA: AltaMira Press, 2000.

Bowers, Tarquin. "Cultivating a Leisurely Life in a Culture of Crowded Time: Rethinking the Work/Leisure Dichotomy." *World Leisure Journal 49, no.* 1 (2007): 30-43.

Brown, Eric. "Contemplative Withdrawal in the Hellenistic Age." *Philosophical Studies* 137 (2008): 79-89.

Buber, Martin. *Between Man and Man*. New York: McMillan, 1965.

———. *The Knowledge of Man: A Philosophy of the Interhuman*. New York: Harper and Row, 1966.

Carr, D. "Maurice Merleau-Ponty: Incarnate consciousness." In *Existential philosophers: Kierkegaard to Merleau-Ponty*. Edited by G. A. Schrader, 369-430. New York: McGraw-Hill, 1967.

Casey, Edward S. On the Issue of Presence. *The Journal of Philosophy. 77, no.*10 (1980): 643-644.

Cushman, Grant, Bob Gidlow. 2008. "A Response to Re-framing Questions: Assessing the Significance of Leisure." *World Leisure Journal 50, no.* 2 (2008): 138-145.

Eagleton, Terry. *Marx*. New York: Routledge, 1999.

Edington, Christopher R. "Leisure: A Framework for policy." *World Leisure Journal 48 no.* 1 (2006): 5-12.

Elster, Jon. *Karl Marx: A Reader*. New York: University of Cambridge, 1986.

Epicurus. "Letter to Menoeceus." In *The Essential Epicurus*. Translated by R. M. Baird, S. E. Rosenbaum, 61-69. New York: Prometheus Books, 1993.

Fish, William. *Philosophy of Perception: A Contemporary Introduction*. New York: Routledge, 2010.

Fromm, Erich. *Marx's Concept of Man*. New York: Frederick Ungar Publishing Co, 1969.

Gadamer, Hans-Georg. *Truth and Method*. 1960. New York: Continuum, 2002.

Guignon, Charles, K. Aho. "Phenomenological Reflections on Work and Leisure in America." In *The Value of Time and Leisure in a World of Work*.

Edited by Mitchell R. Haney, A. David Kline, 25-38. Lanham, MD: Lexington Books, 2010.

Hadot, Pierre. *What is Ancient Philosophy?* 1995. Cambridge, MA: Belknap Harvard University Press, 2004.

———.*Philosophy As A Way of Life*. 1995. Malden, MA: Blackwell Publishing, 2009.

Haney, Mitchell R. "The Value of Slow." In *The Value of Time and Leisure in a World of Work*. Edited by Mitchell R. Haney, A. David Kline, 151-164. Lanham, MD: Lexington Books, 2010.

Heidegger, Martin. *Being and Time*. San Francisco, CA: HarperCollins, 1962.

Henriot, Jacques. *Le Jeu*. Paris: Presses Universitaires de France, 1969.

Hinman, Laurence M. 1978. "Marx's Theory of Play, Leisure, and Unalienated Praxis. *Philosophy and Social Criticism*." 5 (1978): 192-228.

Holba, Annette. "Transformative leisure as Recuperative Praxis: Texturing Human Communication." *World Leisure Journal* 48, no. 1 (2007): 13-23.

———.*Transformative Leisure: Recuperative Praxis for Human Communication*. Milwaukee, WI: Marquette University Press, 2007.

———, Kylo-Patrick R. Hart, K. R. "Introduction." In *Media and the Apocalypse*. Edited by Kylo-Patrick R. Hart, Annette M. Holba, vii-xiv. New York: Peter Lang, 2009.

Husserl, Edmund. *The Crisis of European Sciences and Transcendental Phenomenology: An Introduction to Phenomenological Philosophy*. Evanston, IL: Northwestern University Press, 1970.

Hyde, Michael J. *The Call of Conscience: Heidegger and Levinas, Rhetoric and the Euthanasia Debate*. Columbia, SC: University of South Carolina Press, 2001.

Johnstone, Christopher L. *Listening to the Logos: Speech and the Coming of Wisdom in Ancient Greece*. Columbia, SC: University of South Carolina Press, 2009.

Kant, Immanuel. *The Cambridge Edition of the Works of Immanuel Kant: Practical philosophy*. New York: Cambridge University Press, 1996.

Lasch, Christopher. *The Culture of Narcissism: American Life in An Age of Diminishing Expectation*. New York: Norton, 1979.

Lazare, Bernard. *Anti-Semitism: Its History and Its Causes*. New York: Cosimo Classics, 2005.

Lazare, Bernard. *Jewish Nationalism*. Translated by M. Abidor. *Le Nationalisme Juif*. Paris: Stock, 1898. <http://www.marxists.org/reference/archive/lazare-ernard/1898/jewish-nationalism.htm>. Accessed 1 July 2010.

Levinas, Emmanuel. *Alterity & Transcendence*. Translated by M. B. Smith. New York: Columbia University Press, 1999.

————. *Difficult Freedom: Essays on Judaism*. Baltimore, MD: The Johns Hopkins University Press, 1963.

————. *Entre Nous: Thinking-of-the-Other*. 1991. Translated by M. B. Smith, B. Harshav. New York: Columbia University Press, 1998.

————. *Philosophy and the Idea of the Infinite: An Introduction to the Philosophy of Emmanuel Levinas*. Translated by Adrian Peperzak. West Lafayette, IN: Purdue University Press, 1993.

————. *Totality and Infinity: An Essay on Exteriority*. Trans. Alphonso Lingis. Pittsburgh, PA: Duquesne University Press, 2000.

Lukács, Georg. *History and Class Consciousness*. Cambridge, MA: MIT Press, 1968.

Mannell, Roger. C. "Leisure, Health, and Well-being." *World Leisure Journal* 49, *no*. 3 (2007): 1114-128.

Marx, Karl. *Capital*. 1967. Vol. 1. New York: Penguin Books, 1990.

————. *Grundrisse*. 1939. Harmondsworth: Penguin Books, 1973.

————. *Writings of the Young Marx on Philosophy and Society*. Edited by L. D. Easton, K., H. Guddat. Indianapolis, IN: Hackett Publishing, 1997.

Menuhin, Yehudi. *Unfinished journey: Twenty years later*. Fromm Intl, 1999.

Merleau-Ponty, Maurice. *Phenomenology of Perception*. 1962. London: Routledge & Kegan Paul, 1967.

————. *Primacy of Perception*. 1964. Evanston, IL: Northwestern University Press, 1975.

————. *The structure of behavior*. 1942. Boston: Beacon Press, 1963.

Mickunas, Algis. "Maurice Merleau-Ponty: Communicative Practice." In *Perspectives on Philosophy of Communication*. Edited by Pat Arneson, 139-158. West Lafayette, IN: Purdue University Press, 2007.

Mill, J. S. *Principles of political economy*. 1871. Vol. III. Canada: University of Toronto Press, 1965.

Nietzsche, Friedrich. *On the Genealogy of Morals and Ecce Homo*. New York: Vintage Books, 1967.

O'Neill, John. *Perception, Expression, and History: The Social Phenomenology of Maurice Merleau-Ponty*. Evanston, IL: Northwestern University Press, 1970.

Pais, Jose M. 2006. "The Cult of the Dead and Leisure: Escaping Loneliness." *World Leisure Journal 48, no.* 4 (2006): 11-21.

Pieper, Josef. *A Brief Reader on the Virtues of the Human Heart*. 1988. San Francisco, CA: Ignatius Press, 1991.

―――. *Faith, Hope, Love*. San Francisco, CA: Ignatius Press, 1997.

―――. *The Four Cardinal Virtues*. 1954. Notre Dame, IN: University of Notre Dame Press, 2007.

―――. *In Defense of Philosophy*. 1966. San Francisco, CA: Ignatius Press, 1992.

―――. *Leisure: The Basis of Culture*. 1952. South Bend, IN: St. Augustine Press, 1998.

Pirruccello, Ann. "Interpreting Simone Weil: Presence and Absence in Attention." *Philosophy East and West 45, no.* 1 (1995): 61-72.

Plato. "The Republic." *Great Dialogues of Plato*. Translated by E. H. Warmington, P. G. Rouse, 118-422. NY: Signet Classics, 1984.

Ramsey, Ramsey Eric. "On the Dire Necessity of the Useless: Philosophical and Rhetorical Thoughts on Hermeneutics and Education in the Humanities." In *Education, Dialogue, and Hermeneutics*. Edited by P. Fairfield, 91-105. New York: Continuum, 2011.

―――. *The long path to nearness: A contribution to a corporeal philosophy of communication and the groundwork for an ethics of relief*. New York: Humanity Books, 1998.

―――. "Somehow, Learning to Live: On Being Critical. *Communication and Critical/Cultural Studies 8, no.* 1 (2011): 88-92.

―――, David J. Miller eds. *Experiences between Philosophy and Communication: Engaging the philosophical contributions of Calvin O. Schrag*. New York: SUNY, 2003.

Ricoeur, Paul. *Time and narrative*. vol. 3. Chicago: University of Chicago Press, 1988.

Rojek, Chris. "Did Marx Have a Theory of Leisure?" *Leisure Studies 3* (1984): 163-174.

―――. *The labour of leisure*. Thousand Oaks, CA: Sage, 2010.

Schiller, Friedrich. *Letters upon the aesthetic education of man*. 1794. Whitefish, MT: Kessinger Publishing, 1994.

Schrag, Calvin O. *The Resources of Rationality: A Response to the Postmodern Challenge*. Bloomington, IN: Indiana University Press, 1992.

―――. *The Self After Postmodernity*. New Haven, CT: Yale University Press, 1997.

Schrag, Calvin O., Ramsey Eric Ramsey. "Method and Phenomenological Research: Humility and Commitment in Interpretation." *Human Studies*. 17 (1994): 131-137.

Sennett, Richard. *The Fall of Public Man*. New York: W. W. Norton S Company, 1974.

Shaw, Susan M. "Re-framing Questions: Assessing the Significance of Leisure." *World Leisure Journal 49, no.* 2 (2007): 59-68.

Sokolowski, Robert. *Introduction to Phenomenology*. Cambridge, NY: Cambridge University Press, 2000.

Stanovich, Keith E. *The Robot's Rebellion: Finding Meaning in the Age of Darwin*. Chicago, IL: University of Chicago Press, 2004.

Stewart, John. *Bridges Not Walls: A Book About Interpersonal Communication*. 8th ed. New York: McGraw-Hill, 2002.

Swift, S. *Hannah Arendt*. New York: Routledge, 2009.

Toulmin, Stephen. *Reason in Ethics*. Cambridge: Cambridge University Press, 1968.

Veblen, Thorstein. *Theory of the Leisure Class*. 1899. New York: Mentor Books, 1953.

Vico, Giovanni Battista. *On the Study Methods of Our Time. Translated by* E. Gianturco. Indianapolis: Bobbs-Merrill, 1965.

Weil, Simone. *Gravity and Grace*. London: Routledge, 1952.

―――. *Waiting for God*. New York: Harper and Row, 1973.

Wiener, Linda, Ramsey Eric Ramsey. Leaving Us to Wonder: An Essay on the Questions Science Can't Ask. New York: SUNY, 2005.

Wilde, Oscar. "The Soul of Man Under Socialism." 1891. In *The Soul of Man Under Socialism and Selected Critical Prose*. Edited by L. Dowling, 125-162. New York: Penguin Classics, 2001.

Winter, Richard. *Still Bored in a Culture of Entertainment: Rediscovering Passion and Wonder*. Downers Grove, IL: InterVarsity Press, 2002.

INDEX

Date Due

JAN 0 6 2015		
NOV 1 8 2015		